Conflict:
A Beginner's Guide

"Illuminating and challenging. Caters well for both the newcomer and the old hands who have grown jaded with the current state of conventional wisdom."

Henry Patterson – Professor of Politics, University of Ulster, and author of *Ireland since 1939: The Persistence of Conflict*

"Outstanding. I would certainly recommend it."

Thomas Hennessey – Reader in History, Canterbury Christ Church University, and author of *A History of Northern Ireland, 1920-1996*

"An excellent introduction. It draws on an impressive range of sources and is admirably clear-sighted about the problems that remain in the wake of the 1998 Agreement."

Graham Walker – Professor of Political History, Queen's University Belfast, and author of *A History of the Ulster Unionist Party: Protest, Pragmatism, and Pessimism*

ONEWORLD BEGINNER'S GUIDES combine an original, inventive, and engaging approach with expert analysis on subjects ranging from art and history to religion and politics, and everything in between. Innovative and affordable, books in the series are perfect for anyone curious about the way the world works and the big ideas of our time.

Beginners
GUIDES

The Northern Ireland Conflict

A Beginner's Guide

Aaron Edwards
Cillian McGrattan

ONEWORLD
OXFORD

A Oneworld Paperback Original

Published by Oneworld Publications 2010

Copyright © Aaron Edwards and Cillian McGrattan 2010

ISBN 978-1-85168-729-9

Typeset by Jayvee, Trivandrum, India
Cover design by Simon McFadden
Printed and bound by CPI Cox and Wyman, Reading, RG1 8EX

Oneworld Publications
UK: 185 Banbury Road, Oxford, OX2 7AR, England
USA: 38 Greene Street, 4th Floor, New York, NY 10013, USA
www.oneworld-publications.com

Contents

Acknowledgements

We would like to extend special thanks to Professor Henry Patterson for his support during the writing of this book. Aaron Edwards wishes to thank Stephen Bloomer, Shirley Brace, Catherine Cooke, Michael Doherty, Harry Donaghy, Nigel Gardiner, Jon McCourt, and Syd Trotter for invaluable assistance with chapter 5. He is particularly grateful for the research funding provided by Sean McKnight, the Director of Studies at the Royal Military Academy Sandhurst, which enabled him to visit archival institutions in London and Oxford. Stephen Bloomer, Ed Flint, Ali Parchami, Colin Reid, and Jennifer Ullah also provided much-needed moral support when the heavy teaching load at RMAS threatened to impinge upon research and writing. Cillian McGrattan thanks the School of Politics at the University of Ulster for providing funding for research trips and the staff at the School for their encouragement. He also wishes to thank Sahla Aroussi, who read over an early draft of the Conclusion. While we adhered to a division of labour approach when writing the book it is, above all, a joint effort and we remain equally responsible for any remaining errors.

Chronology

1920   Government of Ireland Act partitions North and South.

1922   Royal Ulster Constabulary (RUC) is formed.

1925   Boundary Commission publishes report, effectively confining the new state to the six north-eastern counties of Fermanagh, Armagh, Tyrone, Londonderry, Antrim, and Down.

1932   Outdoor relief riots see Protestant and Catholic poor join forces to protest against the Unionist government's handling of the unemployment problem.

1935   Prospects for political cooperation between the two communities are shattered when loyalist and republican gunmen embark on a campaign of shooting and bombing, leading to an upsurge in sectarianism.

1940   Death of Lord Craigavon, the first prime minister of Northern Ireland.

1941   April and May: Belfast Blitz, when the German Luftwaffe bombs Belfast.

1943   Sir Basil Brooke takes over as prime minister following the resignation of John Miller Andrews.

1956   December: Irish Republican Army (IRA) border campaign, code-named Operation Harvest, is launched in which republicans attack scores of infrastructural and security force targets across Northern Ireland.

1962   February: The IRA calls a halt to its border campaign citing 'the anathema of Northern nationalist opinion'.

1963   Terence O'Neill takes over as prime minister announcing that he intends to 'transform the face of Ulster'.

1965   November: The Ulster Volunteer Force (UVF) is formed, following the swearing-in of Gusty Spence and his appointment as its first commander. The organisation was initially set up to destabilise Terence O'Neill's liberal regime, which was under heavy pressure from Ian Paisley and his ultra-conservative supporters.

1966   The UVF are responsible for three murders. The organisation declares war on the IRA, which is largely a symbolic, not actual, threat.

1967   January: Northern Ireland Civil Rights Association is launched at a press conference in Belfast.

1968   5 October: Duke Street clashes in Derry City, between civil rights protesters and the RUC, leads to civil disobedience.

1969   April: Terence O'Neill resigns from office, claiming later that he was literally 'bombed from office' by the UVF.

      August: British troops are sent on to the streets in a peacekeeping role. The codename given to the army's Military Aid to the Civil Power (MACP) deployment is Operation Banner. It is anticipated that the deployment will be temporary; it is not ended until 2007.

      December: The IRA splits between those who support armed struggle and those who prefer a political route. Those who remain in the meeting become known as the Official IRA, and those who walk out form the nucleus of the Provisional IRA (PIRA).

1970   January: Sinn Féin splits between Official and Provisional wings. The latter remains subservient to the militarism of the Provisional IRA until the 1980s.

      April: The Alliance Party is formed.

      August: The Social Democratic and Labour Party (SDLP) is formed.

1971   August: Brian Faulkner announces the introduction of internment without trial.

September: The Democratic Unionist Party (DUP) is formed.

1972   January: Civil rights protesters in Derry are shot by soldiers of the First Battalion, the Parachute Regiment. Thirteen people are killed instantly; another man shot on the day dies two weeks later. The outcry from nationalists and republicans across the province galvanises support for the IRA.

March: Edward Heath announces the prorogation of the Stormont administration. Four days later the parliament meets for the last time.

July: Operation Motorman, the British Army's largest single military manoeuvre since the Suez Canal crisis in 1956, is launched to smash so-called 'no go' areas and to reclaim control of the streets from the IRA in Belfast and Londonderry.

1973   March: Government White Paper calls for devolved power sharing and an 'Irish dimension'.

November: Power-sharing executive agreed.

December: Sunningdale communiqué provides for the institutionalisation of an 'Irish dimension' in the form of the Council of Ireland.

1974   May: Ulster Workers' Council strike leads to the collapse of the 'Sunningdale executive'.

1975   Constitutional Convention established to provide a forum for Northern Ireland parties to discuss future political arrangements.

IRA ceasefire and 'secret' talks with the British government; ceasefire holds until the end of the summer.

1976   Constitutional Convention ends.

IRA prisoners refuse to wear prison uniforms.

1977   The PIRA restructure their organisation into cells and settle in for a 'long war'.

1980   May: Margaret Thatcher and Charles Haughey meet

to discuss how Anglo-Irish relations could be improved.

December: First hunger strike called off with one prisoner critically ill.

1981 March: Second hunger strike announced – Bobby Sands is the first prisoner to refuse food.

April: Sands elected MP in Fermanagh-South Tyrone by-election.

May: Sands dies on sixty-sixth day of his strike.

June: Two hunger strikers elected to the Dáil.

October: Hunger strikes called off.

1982 Sinn Féin contest elections for new Northern Ireland Assembly, winning ten per cent of the vote (around one-in-three of Catholic votes). Nationalists boycott the subsequent Assembly.

1984 October: IRA bomb Conservative Party conference hotel in Brighton killing five people, and narrowly missing PM Margaret Thatcher.

1985 November: Margaret Thatcher and Garret FitzGerald sign Anglo-Irish Agreement affording Dublin a consultative role in the affairs of Northern Ireland and providing for a restoration of power sharing – the latter being dependent on local agreement. Around 100,000 unionists gather at Belfast City Hall to protest against the Agreement.

1987 November: French authorities intercept the *Eksund* bearing a large consignment of weapons and explosives from Libya on its way to the IRA. An IRA bomb kills eleven people at a Remembrance Day ceremony in Enniskillen.

1988 January: John Hume and Gerry Adams begin a series of *in camera* meetings. Although the meetings are called off and minutes published in September; they continue secretly into the 1990s.

1989   February: Meetings between political parties in Duisburg, West Germany. Talks collapse over disagreements concerning an institutionalised role for Dublin in any future settlement.

November: Secretary of State for Northern Ireland Peter Brooke states that the IRA could not be militarily defeated.

1990   November: Secretary of State Peter Brooke states that Britain has 'no selfish strategic or economic interest' in Northern Ireland. Margaret Thatcher resigns as prime minister, to be replaced by John Major.

1991   March: Brooke announces a 'three-stranded approach' to take into account relationships between Northern Ireland and Westminster, relationships between Northern Ireland and the Republic, and relationships between the Republic and the UK.

1993   December: Downing Street Declaration published by the two governments. It reiterates the 'principle of consent' and calls on the IRA to renounce violence.

1994   January: Gerry Adams admits that the British government have set IRA decommissioning as a precondition for Sinn Féin entering any future talks.

June: Six Catholics killed in a loyalist attack on a bar in Loughinisland, County Down.

August: IRA declares a 'complete cessation' of its armed campaign.

October: The Combined Loyalist Military Command declares a loyalist ceasefire on behalf of the UVF/RHC (Red Hand Commando) and UDA/UFF (Ulster Defence Association/Ulster Freedom Fighters).

December: Bill Clinton appoints Senator George Mitchell as his economic envoy to Northern Ireland.

1995   January: Northern Ireland Office (NIO) reiterate

decommissioning as a precondition to participation in political talks.

May: Secretary of State Patrick Mayhew meets Gerry Adams in Washington.

October: Taoiseach Albert Reynolds says weapons decommissioning had not been a major British demand in the talks leading to the Downing Street Declaration.

November: The two governments appoint George Mitchell as head of a commission to propose a way out of the decommissioning talks impasse.

1996　January: Mitchell Commission recommends that decommissioning should occur in tandem with the talks process.

February: IRA ceasefire ends when it explodes a bomb in London's Canary Wharf.

July: Orangemen are prevented from marching along the mainly nationalist Garvaghy Road in Portadown, County Armagh. Following intense Protestant rioting, the RUC forces the march along the road – further Catholic rioting ensues.

1997　May: Tony Blair leads New Labour to a massive general election victory.

July: IRA announces another ceasefire.

August: Independent Commission on Decommissioning appointed.

September: Sinn Féin sign up to George Mitchell's principles of non-violence and enter all-party talks.

December: Gerry Adams and Martin McGuinness make their first visit to Downing Street.

1998　10 April: The Good Friday Agreement is signed by all parties to the talks, except the DUP who stage a walkout.

1999　Elections are held to the Stormont Assembly.

2000 August: A bitter internecine feud breaks out between rival loyalists.

2001 The UVF and UDA call a halt to their feud. The bloodletting leaves the position of the dissident Loyalist Volunteer Force (LVF) unresolved.

2002 The Holy Cross dispute, in which loyalists stage a protest at republican men walking young girls to school, raises tensions in the Ardoyne area of North Belfast.

2004 Another feud breaks out between the LVF and the UVF, in which four men are shot dead. The LVF announces that it is leaving the paramilitary stage.

2005 January: IRA members allegedly murder a Catholic man, Robert McCartney, near the Markets area of Belfast. The killing provokes international condemnation and a worldwide campaign for justice by his sisters.

July: The Provisional IRA calls a halt to its campaign and declares its war over.

September: The IRA decommissions the last of its weaponry.

2006 November: The St Andrews Agreement is signed between the British and Irish governments and the main political parties. The DUP announce that they have rewritten the Agreement.

2007 3 May: The UVF announces that it is ending its 'campaign of armed resistance to violent nationalism'.

May: Ian Paisley and Gerry Adams announce the formation of a power-sharing executive, effectively ending the institutional stalemate.

November: The UDA announces that it is to 'stand down' and that 'all weaponry will be put beyond use'.

2008 November: After five months of political deadlock agreement is finally reached between the local parties on the devolution of policing and criminal justice powers to Stormont.

2009 February: Secretary of State Shaun Woodward announces that policing and criminal justice powers will be transferred from Westminster to Stormont, thus fulfilling the British government's commitment under the St Andrews Agreement.

February: Woodward states that the recommendation made by the Commission on the Past in Northern Ireland that the families of each victim of the Troubles should receive £12,000 will not be taken forward. The proposal enraged many people in Northern Ireland by apparently elevating killers to the same status as their victims. The Commission's thirty-plus other recommendations, including a £300 million 'Legacy Commission' are to be given further consideration.

March: Two young soldiers preparing for their imminent deployment to Helmand Province in Afghanistan are mercilessly cut down in a hail of gunfire by dissident Real IRA gunmen. The attack leads to a mass cross-community protest against violence in Belfast city centre not seen since 2002.

June: The UVF and UDA announce that they have placed their 'arms beyond use', thereby signalling loyalist decommissioning.

Note on terminology

The language used to describe the Northern Ireland conflict is often politically loaded, and we have endeavoured to use terms preferred by different groups when describing those groups.

For example, while nationalists refer to Northern Ireland's second largest city as 'Derry', unionists refer to it as 'Londonderry'; nationalists also often refer to Northern Ireland as 'the North' or the 'six counties'.

In order to avoid repetition, we have also referred to the conflict as the 'Troubles', although we acknowledge that this euphemistic colloquialism does not capture adequately the very real suffering endured by many families and individuals.

We have used 'Unionist' to refer to the Ulster Unionist and Democratic Unionist parties, and to the government of Northern Ireland, which was controlled by the Ulster Unionist Party from 1921 to 1972. We reserve the lower-case 'unionist' to refer to the wider political community that favours maintaining constitutional links with the UK. Similarly, we have referred to 'nationalists' in the lower case to refer to the political community that favours ending partition.

Introduction

For more than a generation Northern Ireland was a byword for sectarian conflict, terrorism, and civil disobedience. The sound of gun-fire and explosions rang out across the world, leading many contemporaries to wonder if 'the Troubles' were truly insoluble. Yet, as we glance back over the course of the past half century, the Northern Ireland conflict cuts a familiar, almost banal, silhouette when illuminated against the backdrop of current global and regional instability. While we can debate the finer points of scale, the dark history of this bloody conflict continues to cast a long shadow.

Despite this reputation, the Northern Ireland conflict has been transformed beyond violence over the past decade, and especially since a power-sharing administration was formed in 2007 by the region's two dominant, yet diametrically opposing, political parties: the Democratic Unionist Party (DUP) and Sinn Féin. Despite the bedding-down of the new executive and Assembly, there remains some controversy over whether the 1998 Belfast/Good Friday Agreement paved the way for this eventual transformation.[1] Political engagement between these once implacable enemies has been played out against a backdrop of fundamental change in the relationships within and between the unionist and nationalist communities. The de-escalation of the military dimension of the conflict since the early 1990s certainly added the necessary lubricant to the wheels of what former Prime Minister Tony Blair called 'the settlement train', but it does not explain *why* the idea of peace captured the imagination of so many when it did, or *how* it has lasted for so long. From a conflict which at its height saw up to 30,000 British soldiers deployed on the streets to provide military aid to the civil power, to the ruthless long-running paramilitary campaigns perpetrated by loyalist and republican groups, Northern Ireland has since become a model for successful peace and reconciliation processes elsewhere. This book explains what made compromise possible in one of the most bitter and protracted conflicts of modern times.

Conflict in Northern Ireland: a familiar story?

Between 1966 and 2003 the euphemistically titled 'Troubles' claimed 3703 lives. Around 40,000 other people were seriously wounded as a direct result of hostilities. Unsurprisingly, given the small population of around 900,000 Protestants and 600,000 Catholics, few people remained untouched by the violence and inter-communal mistrust, fear, and hatred which marred Northern Irish society for four decades. Political stalemate persisted during these years as Protestants, who mostly voted for Ulster Unionist political parties (such as the Ulster Unionist Party (UUP) or the DUP), favoured maintaining the constitutional link with the UK, while Catholics, who mostly voted for Irish Nationalist parties (such as the Social Democratic and Labour Party (SDLP) and Sinn Féin), aspired to a united Ireland.

While the figure of almost 4000 deaths may appear small when placed in absolute terms against other conflicts, proportionally, it would translate as around 100,000 deaths in the UK or 500,000 in the United States – around ten times the number of Americans killed in Vietnam.[2] Militant nationalists or Irish Republicans, whose key paramilitary organisation was the Irish Republican Army (IRA), accounted for just under sixty per cent of those deaths. Militant unionists in the form of loyalist paramilitaries accounted for around thirty per cent of the fatalities, while the state security forces, the Royal Ulster Constabulary (RUC) and the British Army contributed to the remainder.[3]

As peace takes root it is undoubtedly becoming difficult for younger generations to appreciate how, for most of the past forty years, Northern Ireland stood at a crossroads, with the prospect of peace a much more distant option for two communities deeply divided along ethnic, national, religious, cultural, and class lines. Throughout the 1990s the embryonic peace process was nurtured by community leaders on all sides and at all levels – from statesmen to church leaders, to reformed (and reforming paramilitaries) and ordinary people – who found the slaughter of innocent civilians repugnant and wished to do something about it. Many of those who lobbied long and hard for peace had themselves contributed to the armed conflict in the region in more damaging ways through political obfuscation and the manipulation of ethnic sentiments. While they continue to stand firm as implacable enemies, they have now chosen to put aside their differences and engage with one another through the conduit of political dialogue and debate.

Politics is not just something that is practised at the elite level of society, by experienced politicians clamouring around a well-polished negotiating table in arcane mansion houses or in the squeaky-clean corridors of power in Belfast, London, or elsewhere, but is firmly grounded in the local communities which bore the brunt of the violent conflict. It may be something of a cliché to admit, but US Democratic Speaker of the House of Representatives, Tip O'Neill's famous observation that 'all politics is local' is nonetheless apt: the intensity of hatred and mistrust in grass-roots communities has huge repercussions at a national and international level.

This book is also about the complex processes which served to bring about a transformation in the Northern Ireland conflict and how each level of society contributed to building peace. It focuses on the multi-layered government of the region, from the former Stormont administration run entirely by Unionists with the retention of the province within the UK uppermost in the minds of its leaders, to the new power-sharing administration which claims to govern on behalf of all of the people.

Terrorism, the state, and international security

Curiously the main parties in conflict have resisted the temptation to label the conflict as a 'war'. Indeed, the DUP successfully passed a motion by forty-six votes to twenty in the newly reconstituted Northern Ireland Assembly in 2008, calling on members to recognise: 'That this Assembly repudiates any suggestion that the 30 year terrorist campaign in Northern Ireland be re-classified as a "war".' As one DUP Assembly Member observed in the debating chamber, 'We know that the IRA did not fight a war – for they ignored the international conventions that govern warfare.' Yet, the principal terrorist groups, such as the IRA and the Ulster Volunteer Force (UVF), did declare war on each other and, in the case of the former, on the British presence in Ireland. Indeed, Irish republican terrorist groups pioneered in many of the tactics and techniques subsequently utilised by terrorists and insurgents around the globe, including improvised explosive devices, assassinations of government ministers and civilians, the blitzing of commercial centres, as well as naked sectarian killings. Loyalist groups also inflicted heavy casualties on those whom they regarded as their enemy – as with republicans, in many cases this meant innocent, defenceless civilians.

The end of the Cold War (1989–91) between the rival superpowers of the United States and the Soviet Union brought with it an upsurge in ethnic quarrels as many former Communist satellite states broke away. Yet in more established democracies, where terrorism had been commonplace, the opposite was true. Throughout the 1990s there was an upsurge in inter-ethnic violence, especially in the Balkans and Sub-Saharan Africa, as inter-ethnic, tribal, and clan tensions led to intra-state conflict. Amidst the violence, however, peace processes did take root, if only temporarily, in Israel–Palestine, Northern Ireland and South Africa. Both Northern Ireland and South Africa became models for the peaceful resolution of protracted violence in other divided societies.

Moreover, broader fluctuations in the international arena after the attacks on the United States on 11 September 2001 made it less than propitious for groups to employ the indiscriminate method of terrorism to pursue their political goals. The acceptance by the main parties that violence could serve no useful purpose in achieving political goals found more adherents after the end of the Cold War. However, it was to take many more years before peace finally bedded down and a political settlement won over its most vocal opponents. In the context of what Mary Kaldor has called 'new wars', where differences between cultures, traditions, and beliefs form a major component of division between peoples, the Northern Ireland conflict is far from unique.[4] What distinguishes Northern Ireland from other places plagued by conflict is not that it involves separatist and conservative, or anti- and pro-state groups; rather, it is the specific coincidence of those factors with the specific decisions and omissions that were made on the ground.

The attempts to find a way out of those troubled histories cannot be exported as some sort of skeleton key that will unlock the puzzle of all ethnic, racial, religious, or nationalist quarrels. Just as the conflict emerged and persisted according to the particular way in which various actors responded (or omitted to respond), and the methods armed groups utilised to conduct their hostilities, the Northern Ireland peace process should not be seen as a model to be followed: what worked in one context may not work in another. Certainly there are similarities – as this book will endeavour to highlight – between the Irish conflict and those that continue to plague the world today and may continue to do so in the future. However, at its very core the Northern Ireland conflict is a political one. As in other regions bedevilled by terrorism, insurgency, and state-based violence, a political solution can be found.

The Northern Ireland conflict revisited

This book is a historical re-imaging of the Northern Ireland conflict. It uses recently released and otherwise unpublished archival material to revisit what has been a critical period in Anglo-Irish history. This untapped material allows us to question the continued relevance of received wisdom about the conflict. Silencing the voices of those who did not emerge as the dominant players in the aftermath of war and armed conflict has long been the preserve of victors. However, simply repeating tired truisms will not do. An example of this is the oft-repeated quotation from Winston Churchill, who told the House of Commons in 1922 that:

> Great Empires have been overturned. The whole map of Europe has been changed. The position of countries has been violently altered. The modes of thought of men, the whole outlook on affairs, the grouping of parties, all have encountered violent and tremendous changes in the deluge of the world; but as the deluge of the waters subsides and the waters fall short, we

see the dreary steeples of Fermanagh and Tyrone emerging once again.

The idea that the eruption of violent conflict in Northern Ireland at the end of the 1960s was an inevitable result of centuries-old antagonisms is superficially attractive. What that ethnic explanation fails to do, however, is to say why the violence occurred in the way it did; why it occurred when it did; and why it persisted for over three decades. Furthermore, by continuing blandly to reproduce stories about ethnic antagonisms, there is a risk that the explanations we leave to future generations will simply recycle the stories and the myths that fed the conflict and thereby postpone a long-hoped-for resolution.

This book is the result of a deliberate historical and political choice made by the authors to avoid recourse to stories about ancient 'ethno-nationalist antagonisms' and, instead, to concentrate on the historical and political choices made during the conflict. It takes a broad chronological approach, exploring several themes and events with reference to the most up-to-date thinking and research on 'the Troubles' in Ireland.

Chapter 1 explains the background to the conflict from the formation of the Northern Ireland state in the early 1920s. It details the nature of Unionist Party authority in the region, its main opponents, and how challenges by the paramilitary campaigns led to the unravelling of the state by 1972. Chapter 2 looks at the aftermath of the British government's intervention and the subsequent attempt to try to set up a devolved power-sharing administration in the form of the short-lived 'Sunningdale executive'. Chapter 3 examines the entrenchment of the division in the late 1970s and the increasingly inter-governmental approach of the 1980s. Chapter 4 looks at the aftermath of the 1985 Anglo-Irish Agreement and the beginnings of the peace process. Chapter 5 investigates the political deadlock that set in almost immediately following the signing of the Good Friday Agreement and asks: in the absence of institutional compromise, how did local communities deal with the vacuum caused by this stalemate? It argues that, above all, the institutional stalemate left community relations practitioners to manage conflict on the interfaces where antagonism was at its sharpest. This chapter paints a vivid picture of violence as both communities confronted one another. Chapter 6 complements this thematic approach by dissecting the explanations offered about the Northern Ireland conflict. The Conclusion ties together the key themes and events explored in the book by focusing on how the legacy of past violence is being dealt with by people in Northern Ireland and what the prospects actually are for peaceful co-existence between the two communities in the future.

1

The origins of the conflict, 1921–72

Partition and the birth of the state

The Northern Ireland state was formed between 1920 and 1922, at a time when the British government was recovering from a massive drain on its financial coffers caused by having fought a catastrophic total war. The effects of World War I were far reaching across Europe. In Germany, Communist and Fascist groups arose, backed by the muscle of demobilised soldiers and disgruntled unemployed workers, and jostled with one another in the streets against the backdrop of diminished authority exhibited by the Weimar Republic's social democratic government. Meanwhile, the Union of Soviet Socialist Republics (USSR) was born out of the Bolsheviks' bloody seizure of power in 1917, while the Ottoman Empire perished amidst the chaotic turmoil of an Arab revolt and the rise of ethnic nationalism. A similar fate overtook the Austrian-Hungarian Empire, which dissolved in 1918 following military defeat in World War I. From Constantinople to Berlin old certainties were overturned, regimes rocked and toppled, and battle scars were left across the world. Ireland did not remain insulated for long from the revolutionary and counter-revolutionary forces setting the Continent ablaze. Despite the collapse of three imperial dynasties, the British Empire continued to extend its frontiers, most notably when the League of Nations allocated Britain responsibility for the mandated territories of Iraq,

Palestine, and Transjordan,[1] although the government was seeking ways to contract its obligations closer to home.

Fearful of similar turmoil taking root, Unionist politicians elected to the newly established Northern Ireland Parliament in 1921 attempted to erect bulwarks against what they saw as the 'twin evils' of communism and republicanism, marshalling all available resources at their disposal to quell dissent among the working classes.[2] The Ulster Unionist Party (UUP) saw this as the perfect opportunity to strengthen its control over the local administration. Representing the majority Ulster Protestant tradition in the north-east counties of Ireland, the Unionists had won the first elections to the local parliament by a comfortable majority. In British eyes partition was an effective way of managing a conflict many in London viewed as a curiosity; in this instance it would copper-fasten the Union while staving off any further complications in Ireland.

BACKGROUND TO THE CONFLICT

Nationalists and unionists are divided over the basic causes and proposed solutions to the Northern Ireland conflict. Nationalists, for example, often date the conflict to the Anglo-Norman invasion of 1169 and point to subsequent key events to illustrate Britain's oppressive role in Irish history and the frequent resistance by the Irish. Events such as the massacres and repression by Cromwell during the 1640s, the suppression of the United Irishmen Rebellion during the 1790s, the Famine years of the 1840s, and the execution of the leaders of the 1916 Easter Rising serve as critical reference points in that nationalist narrative. The unionist historical narrative is also marked by key events such as the massacres of Protestants at the hands of Catholics in 1641, the victory of King William of Orange over the Catholic King James II in 1690, the resistance to British attempts to impose 'Home Rule' in 1912–14 and the sacrifices of the Ulster Division during the Battle of the Somme in 1916.

BACKGROUND TO THE CONFLICT (*cont.*)

For unionists, these events illustrate a history of Catholic oppression and betrayal and Protestant loyalty to the Crown and the Union. The 'siege mentality' fostered by that history is often expressed in the slogan 'No surrender'.

British attempts to cut off or 'insulate' Westminster politics from the 'Irish question' reached a high point in the late nineteenth and early twentieth centuries with the idea of 'Home Rule', in which a Dublin parliament would rule Ireland but would still be ultimately answerable to London. During the 1910s these attempts coincided with – and, to a large extent, inspired – a growing militarisation and radicalisation of Irish society. The growing gulf between the two sides was illustrated in the War of Independence fought by the Irish Republican Army against the British (1919–21) and the mobilisation of Protestant support to defend the Union in the North. The British 'solution' to the problem was to impose a settlement that neither side really wanted – partition the thirty-two counties of Ireland into the twenty-six in the south that had a Catholic-nationalist majority and the six in the north that had a Protestant-unionist majority, each to be governed by devolved parliaments in Dublin and Belfast respectively.

The Northern Ireland state was a unique construct in that it reinforced the power of Ulster Protestants, who held a majority share of the population in the six counties in the north-east of Ireland, but who were a minority community in the island of Ireland, with their demographic roots in the Plantation migrants who had crossed to Ireland in the seventeenth century. The Ulster Protestants became dominant in this area. What made the north-east counties so different from the rest of Ireland was their close proximity to Great Britain, a heavy industrial base concentrated in the Lagan Valley in Belfast, and unfettered access to the financial markets of the British Empire. As the Unionist leader Edward Carson proclaimed in 1916: 'it was an "utter fallacy" for the economically incompetent south and west of Ireland to wish to rule the North'.[3] Arguably, there was an economic logic to partition and, when combined with the uneven development of capitalism in Ireland, it was bound to have an effect on the type of society built up in the region.

Northern nationalists, who comprised about a third of the population of the newly formed state, desired an end to partition, and remained highly ambivalent about participating in the state's social and political structures. In fact, the architecture of the political structures guaranteed nationalist disquiet: the initial proportional electoral system was replaced in 1925 by a majoritarian, first-past-the-post arrangement meaning that nationalists could hope for no more than ten to twelve of the fifty-two Stormont Parliament seats at any election. This situation was exacerbated by the re-drawing of electoral boundaries – particularly at the local government level – to ensure Unionist majorities. Gerrymandering, as this practice is known, had a profound effect on Nationalist politics in Northern Ireland. In 1920, for example, there existed twenty-five Nationalist-controlled councils; however, by 1925 – due to the abolition of proportional representation and the rigging of electoral wards – these had been reduced to four. Crucially, Derry City, despite its large Nationalist majority, comprising around sixty-five per cent of the population, was run by a Unionist-dominated corporation until 1968.[4] From the 1930s onwards, nationalists instead looked to the Irish Free State in the south to improve their situation and formed what effectively became 'a state within a state'.[5]

In many respects state-building was a protracted process in Northern Ireland and relied heavily on the professionalism of the local civil service, an organisation equally divided in its bureaucratic tendencies between populist and anti-populist interest groups centred round Unionism's principal leaders.[6] Populists tended to use patronage at their disposal to curry favour among their supporters, many of whom held positions of social rank in the Protestant community. Conversely, anti-populists resisted the temptation to place loyalty above a commitment to a more meritocratic ethos commonly found in Great Britain. Populists complained bitterly about the appointment of Catholics to government posts and preferred to fill gaps in the province's bureaucratic system through a dual-edged process of cronyism and discrimination. Extraneous factors such as socio-economic upheaval played havoc with the local economy, which was already reeling from the stress placed upon it by war-time demands. Unemployment in the province rocketed in the 1920s and reached an incredible twenty per cent by the middle of the decade. This severely affected the local workforce, who exercised their right to protest by downing tools and balloting for strikes, a tactic which serve to cripple the economy still further. The Unionist government appealed to ethnic unity as a means of offsetting the labourist sympathies of a hungry working class. Yet nothing could stymie the challenges now evident within the Protestant community, from both Independent Unionists and, after 1924, the Northern Ireland Labour Party (NILP).

Unionist resilience in the face of such challenges soon proved resurgent. The local regime was greatly aided in its strategy of divide and rule by the upsurge in sectarian tensions and political violence across Belfast. In 1920–2 between 452 and 463 people were killed and 1100 injured as the province became subject to the brinkmanship of rival paramilitary gangs.[7] Several clandestine organisations emerged amidst the calamity of armed conflict precipitated by state formation and included the Irish Republican Army (IRA), supported by the newly established government in Dublin, and the Ulster Volunteer Force (UVF), which was soon to be absorbed into the local security force apparatus. Despite most Protestants being unionist in their political viewpoint not all were convinced that the state's new political masters were competent in their handling of social and economic affairs. On the other hand, there were others who thought that the new regime was too weak-kneed in the face of socialist and republican opposition. The Unionist government was to remain, until its eventual collapse in March 1972, a hostage to these conflicting tendencies.

CONSERVATIVE UNIONISM: THE ULSTER UNIONIST PARTY

The UUP was formed in 1905 to resist attempts by Westminster governments to impose Home Rule on Ireland and to protect Protestant interests. Although the establishment of Northern Ireland represented something of a set-back to the first objective, the party quickly adapted to the new arrangement – aided by the fact that it comprised the majority in the devolved parliament.

Although nationalists often question the ambiguous relationship between the UUP and the more extreme elements within the broad unionist family, UUP politicians and supporters point to the fact that it frequently served to restrain loyalist violence. Likewise, while nationalists point to instances of misrule and discrimination by the UUP-led Northern Irish governments, supporters of the party claimed that the real agenda of Northern nationalists remained reunification rather than civil rights. Indeed, the actions of UUP leaders such as Terence O'Neill during the 1960s, Brian Faulkner during the 1970s, and David Trimble during the 1990s and 2000s strongly suggest a conservative or 'gradualist' approach to change and reform – as distinct from the wholesale, far-reaching proposals advocated at different times by nationalists and republicans.

The split in the Unionist government between populists and anti-populists persisted throughout the 1930s, Unionist prime ministers frequently acting on the basis of what they thought was best for their Protestant working-class supporters. For example, both Sir James Craig and his successor John Miller Andrews were populist in their outlook, while Sir Basil Brooke and his successor Terence O'Neill added a distinctly anti-populist flavour to their style of government in later years. Such division reinforced the disagreement over the exact political strategy to be adhered to by Unionists during these years, an internal dispute that would persist through later generations.

Despite these religious and political divisions, the 'outdoor relief riots' of 1932 brought together Protestants and Catholics to protest against the inequitable treatment handed out to them by the Belfast Poor Law Guardians – the body that was appointed to administer relief to unemployed workers and their families. By 1934, the working classes marched the streets of Belfast in radical unison, with a mainly Protestant Shankill Road contingent making the annual pilgrimage to Bodenstown cemetery in County Kildare for rousing anti-British speeches at the graveside of the eighteenth-century republican martyr Wolfe Tone. However, within a matter of months the potential for cross-sectarian harmony was undermined when a murder campaign by loyalist paramilitaries threatened to shatter the brittle rigidity of solidarity fostered among Protestant and Catholic workers. Predictably, sectarian rioting followed the annual Orange Order parades in Belfast in July 1935. Catholics soon came to view themselves as a besieged minority in a hostile society.[8]

The death of James Craig (Lord Craigavon), Northern Ireland's first prime minister, in November 1940, sent shock-waves throughout the Unionist community. He was succeeded by John Miller Andrews – brother of renowned *Titanic* architect Thomas Andrews – who preferred to take a more conciliatory attitude towards industrial militancy after 1941. At a time when British politicians increasingly questioned the province's contri-bution to the war effort, Andrews' policies left many of his colleagues uneasy and soon proved politically fatal. Northern Ireland alone accounted for ten per cent of the total number of days lost to strikes in the UK, while accounting for only two per cent of industrial output.[9] Andrews resigned as prime minister in

MILITANT LOYALISM: THE UVF

Militant loyalism is often characterised as the least respectable component of the Ulster Unionist political project, yet it has been around since before the third Home Rule crisis of 1910–14. Retired British Army officers were complicit in the raising of the original UVF as a paramilitary army to oppose the possibility of Home Rule government for Ireland. The UVF was staffed by many serving British Army NCOs and officers and was later subsumed into the 36th (Ulster) Division, which fought on the Western Front in World War I. In 1920 the UVF's commanding officer, Lieutenant-General Sir George Richardson, issued an order disbanding the UVF and calling upon its men to disperse into the ranks of the newly constituted Ulster Special Constabulary. The old UVF was consigned to the history books.

The modern UVF was raised in late 1965, when Gusty Spence, a recently demobbed soldier and Belfast shipyard worker, was sworn into the organisation near Pomeroy. The UVF carried out a number of attacks in 1966 – including three killings – but its campaign fizzled out and its leading lights, including Spence, were imprisoned. The UVF remained in the shadows until 1971, when it embarked on a renewed recruiting drive and bombing campaign. Its attack on McGurk's bar, in which fifteen civilians were killed, and its subsequent co-ordinated bomb attacks in Dublin and Monaghan (killing thirty-three), marked it out as a ruthless terrorist organisation. Despite nationalist and republican protestations that it was directly controlled by the British state, the truth was that it remained an autonomous outworking of fear, hatred, and insecurity among the Protestant grass roots. The UVF benefited from the expertise of scores of personnel who had served in the ranks of the British Army in the post-war conflicts in Palestine, Malaya, Aden, and Cyprus, and its propaganda maintained that it was fighting a 'counter-terrorist' campaign against the IRA. The UVF (together with its satellite grouping, the Red Hand Commando (RHC)) was responsible for the deaths of almost 500 people between 1966 and 2004, most of whom were Catholic civilians.[10] The end of its armed campaign was announced by Spence in May 2007, and the UVF and RHC finally decommissioned their weapons in June 2009.

1943, allowing his Minister of Commerce Sir Basil Brooke, the nephew of the Chief of the Imperial General Staff Sir Alan Brooke, to take his place. As a former British Army officer himself, Brooke took a more military approach to prime ministerial matters in Belfast. In his later years there was much criticism that he spent more time on his private estate in Fermanagh than behind his desk or in the parliamentary debating chamber. Northern Ireland politics remained something of an amateurish affair as the Belfast Parliament met infrequently, with many politicians attending on an ad hoc basis.

War and welfarism

The emergence of leftist politics that inspired Clement Atlee's Labour Party landslide victory of July 1945 also affected the stagnant political culture of Northern Ireland. There, the signif-icant electoral outcome was not so much the impressive NILP vote of thirty-two per cent, but the fact that the Nationalist Party was banished from Belfast altogether; a nationalist would not be elected in the city again until the late 1960s. In addition, more than any other government up until that point, the Attlee administration would exert a profound and long-term effect on Northern Irish politics. The main consequence of the establish-ment of the welfare state was that it gave Catholics an incentive to participate in the structures of Northern Ireland for the first time. In time these tangible benefits – as well as growing mater-ial prosperity – would influence Catholic calls for civil rights in the 1960s. Implicitly, it also tied Westminster more closely to the socio-economic well-being of Northern Ireland by requir-ing an increase in service provision, which was historically below the level of the rest of the UK.

However, these changes were not immediately felt – neither on the ground nor at elite level. In 1946, for example, Attlee refused to tackle the dominant Unionist Party head on, choosing instead to offer only half-hearted support to the only official British Labour Party candidate ever to stand in Northern Ireland:

> At the General Election last July the great swing to the Labour Party was much less pronounced in Northern Ireland than in other parts of the United Kingdom, but I feel sure that the cause of Labour is steadily gaining ground in Northern Ireland as it is in so many other parts of these islands. I therefore wish you all success in this by-election.[11]

Powerful grandees in the Labour government like Herbert Morrison became implacable supporters of the Unionists following Germany's surrender in May 1945. In contrast to Dublin's neutrality in World War II, British ministers were convinced that the province had made an invaluable contribution to the war effort – sentiments that were compounded by the recognition of Northern Ireland's vital geo-strategic position in the post-war dispensation.

The British Labour Party itself was staffed by several key figures who believed strongly in the link with Northern Ireland. Party Secretary Morgan Phillips ensured a sympathetic hearing for the province's majority unionist population among Labour's rank-and-file membership, while Attlee and his ministers could rely on the unionist complexion of the civil service to toe the party's line of being broadly supportive of the Unionist government in Belfast. This was especially true in the wake of the Eire government's decision to leave the Commonwealth and establish an Irish Republic in 1948–9. Brooke asked Attlee to ensure that Northern Ireland's status would remain unchanged and the Ireland Bill was drawn up accordingly. A secret government briefing note on the Bill, which was circulated to all government ministers read:

United Kingdom Ministers [will] avoid entering into controversy in elections for the Northern Ireland Parliament, which
are matters for the Government and Parliament of Northern
Ireland.[12]

In other government briefings it was clear that the arguments
advanced in a renewed campaign by Irish nationalists to broaden
the basis of the anti-partitionist lobby were failing to raise
widespread support. These briefings explicitly rejected the idea
that Ireland was an indivisible unit; they also highlighted the
UK's obligations under the North Atlantic Treaty (signed in
April 1949) and pointed to the fact that reunification would
have created severe financial problems for Northern Ireland:

It seems clear that Northern Ireland business interests would be
prejudiced by entering the Southern Irish economy and the
Northern Ireland working man would experience a drop in his
standard of living.[13]

NORTHERN REPUBLICANISM: THE IRA AND SINN FÉIN

Northern Irish nationalists have traditionally been divided into two
groups – constitutional nationalists, who favour gradual, democratic
change, and physical force republicans, who advocate immediate
constitutional change, if needs be, by force. Founded in 1905, Sinn
Féin has acted as the main political party of Irish republicanism in
Northern Ireland, with a key tactic being abstention from what it
viewed as partitionist political structures. Although Sinn Féin
advocated broad left-wing policies, national reunification has traditionally taken priority over issues such as workers' rights or gender
equality. Since at least 1998, Sinn Féin has advocated a more accommodative, 'constitutional nationalist' stance, recognising the validity
of what is known as the 'principle of consent' – namely, that a majority in Northern Ireland must assent to any constitutional change.

The economic arguments underlying the unionist position had been employed by advocates of the continued maintenance of the link with Great Britain since the three Home Rule crises of the late nineteenth and early twentieth centuries. They were articulated most forcefully by Unionist politicians throughout the existence of the local state and would continue to retain their relevance even in the face of a renewed IRA insurgency in the late 1950s and early 1960s.

The IRA's border war, 1956–62

On the night of 10 December 1956 the IRA launched a co-ordinated series of attacks on a range of military, police, and infrastructural targets in rural areas across Northern Ireland. Code-named Operation Harvest it was primarily a military campaign aimed at de-stabilising the Northern Unionist government. Since the end of the Anglo-Irish War of Independence of 1919–21 republican violence had occasionally flared up at impromptu moments, despite the organisation being banned on both sides of the Irish border. In 1939–45 the IRA campaign sought to work in conjunction with the Nazi regime to mount attacks in several British cities. The collaboration of Nazi sympathisers in the IRA has been largely underplayed by subsequent generations of republicans, yet it was presented by the organisation as a way to attack its enemies in Britain while the country remained fixated on a total war with Germany. The IRA bombing campaign during World War II led to the internment of hundreds of suspected IRA volunteers for subversion. The IRA lingered on in the late 1940s and early 1950s, relaunching its activities in 1956 under the direction of its military chief Sean Garland. In a statement released by the IRA's political wing, Sinn Féin, republicans claimed, 'Irishmen have again risen in armed revolt against British aggression in Ireland.' The statement appealed to the Irish people to assist the IRA in its campaign.

When the IRA launched its border offensive against the Northern Ireland state it did so in unfavourable circumstances. Radical republicanism no longer seemed convincing to nationalists in the context of the welfare state. The organisation had not changed its strategy since 1921 and settled into the tactic of harassing the security forces in isolated border outposts. It was not that the IRA particularly lacked men of experience: three of the seven members of its ruling 'army council' had served in the ranks of the British armed forces and were more than proficient with guns and explosives. One of the most daring raids undertaken by the IRA was on a British Army barracks in Aborfield, Berkshire, in August 1955. However, the heavily laden van used to aid their escape was later intercepted by the police who quickly tracked down and arrested its occupants.

INTERNMENT

Internment, or the detention of suspects without trial, had been used at various points in the history of the Northern state by the Stormont government when the threat by republicans was deemed most serious – notably in the early 1920s, during the 'Border campaign' of 1950–62, and in 1971. While the introduction of internment was a factor in the defeat of the IRA's 1950s campaign, this was only true insofar as it was also introduced in the south of Ireland. This cooperation was absent in August 1971, however, when the decision by the Unionist Prime Minister Brian Faulkner to introduce internment proved to be a political disaster – of the 342 suspects arrested all were Catholics and many were maltreated and brutalised when in custody. Nationalist alienation from the state was near total and many Catholic households embarked upon a rent-and-rates strike in protest. Indeed, the international embarrassment caused by the failure of internment to improve the political situation was a decisive factor in the British decision to assume direct control over the North the following March.

Operation Harvest caused widespread consternation among the Protestant community. Several border Protestants warned Lord Brookeborough privately that they would take vigilante action against known IRA members if the government did not act swiftly to counter the threat. This prompted him to make a speech to the Northern Ireland House of Commons, in which he said:

> I am sure that the people of Northern Ireland, the most loyal and sensible people in the world, in spite of the provocation they have had ... will realise that the defence of the country must rest with the Government and that no one should take any action on his own, action which might be detrimental to the welfare of himself and of his fellow men.[14]

One of the inbuilt mechanisms upon which state power rested was the monopoly over the legitimate use of force. The 'B Specials', a reserve police force traditionally viewed with great suspicion by nationalists, was one such component of the security apparatus that served to bring on board even the most militant Ulster Protestants. Responding to grass-roots pressure, Brookeborough talked tough and threatened to draw on the Special Powers Act to tackle the terrorist challenge. The Special Powers Act permitted the local authorities to intern suspects without trial, to impose curfews, and to ban organisations and publications deemed to be subversive by the local administration. 'We have these measures continually under review,' Brookeborough said, 'and if we feel there is the least need for it we will not hesitate to take additional powers.' Within a matter of days the Unionist leadership introduced internment without trial, a punitive action aimed at arresting and detaining IRA suspects.[15]

Despite its call to arms, Operation Harvest failed to generate support and the campaign eventually fizzled out. Militarily it was a disaster: internment was introduced on both sides of the border, severely constraining the IRA's freedom of movement. In the end the campaign accomplished nothing, except to precipitate a fundamental rethink in certain republican circles about their strategic direction: recognising the lack of Northern nationalist support, the republican leadership began to look to civil rights demands to create a cross-community alliance and pressurise the Stormont government for reforms.

DEMOCRATIC SOCIALISM AND SECTARIANISM: THE NORTHERN IRELAND LABOUR PARTY

The NILP was formed in 1924 in the wake of the successful return to power of the first British Labour government under Ramsay McDonald. The NILP won a number of council seats in the 1920s and 1930s, drawing support from both Protestants and Catholics. Paddy Agnew won the seat of South Armagh in the Northern Ireland Parliament in 1938. Although he lost his seat in 1945 the NILP regained two seats in Belfast Dock and Belfast Oldpark and held them between 1945 and 1949. The most successful period for the NILP came in 1958, when it secured four seats at Stormont and became the official opposition. Although two of its MPs, Billy Boyd and David Bleakley, lost their seats in predominantly Protestant areas in 1965, the party held the constituencies of Belfast Pottinger and Belfast Oldpark, which had a significant Catholic voting population. The NILP won around 100,000 first preference votes in both the 1964 and 1970 British general elections, but by the mid 1970s its electoral support haemorrhaged as many of its activists and supporters left to join a plethora of other political and paramilitary organisations. An unfortunate mix of sectarian violence, voter apathy, a new electoral system, and the proliferation of new parties contributed to the NILP's demise and it officially wound up in 1987.[16]

Civil rights

In 1958 the Nationalist Party, supported by the NILP, introduced a resolution at Stormont 'recognising that Northern
Ireland is the only part of these islands which denies universal
adult suffrage in local government elections'. Ten years later, the
same problem was the touchstone of a mass movement that
precipitated the collapse of the Northern state. For while the
principle of 'one person, one vote' was in place for Westminster
elections, at the Stormont and local government levels
labyrinthine regulations linked voting to property. Unionist
elites were conscious of the overt class bias: thus, the then Chief
Whip, Brian Faulkner, gave a 'steer' to grass-roots supporters to
quench working-class discontent:

> We cannot publicise our views on this matter. The reasons are
> quite obvious … the Unionist Party and Government [is]
> safeguarding the position of the Loyalists of Ulster. The
> Socialists can go out on the highways and by-ways and air their
> views but if we were to allow universal suffrage … we may lose
> Derry City and … could lose Fermanagh.[17]

The franchise was intricately linked to gerrymandering, which,
as mentioned above, had its roots in the troubled early 1920s,
when Sir James Craig's government sought to consolidate its
control of the nationalist-dominated border areas of Tyrone,
Fermanagh, and Derry City. The system of domination was
reinforced through a misallocation of houses in key wards and a
disproportionate representation of Catholics in public employment. For example, Catholics made up sixty-one per cent of
Omagh's population, yet returned only nine of the twenty-one
councillors. This was possibly due to the fact that Unionist
majorities were artificially maintained in the town's north and
south wards, which returned six councillors each. Thus, in the
period since World War II, 100% of the houses built in the

north ward and ninety-five per cent in the south ward went to Protestants. In the mainly Nationalist west ward (allocated nine council seats) ninety-eight per cent of houses were given to Catholics.

The situation was repeated across Northern Ireland. In Lurgan, for example, a Catholic population of forty-six per cent, returned none of the fifteen-person council. Armagh's Catholic population constituted 53.5% of the town's population in 1961, but returned eight councillors to the Unionist Party's twelve. Again, of the 205 positions in Tyrone County Council, eight were filled by Catholics; the Lurgan Borough Council employed 156 persons, of whom Catholics totalled twenty-five (twenty-three of whom were labourers); again, of Armagh County Council's 201 non-manual employees, eight were Catholics (no Catholic held a senior position). Historians have sought to contextualise these anomalies, pointing to Stormont's *overall* creditable record of house-building. In addition, Catholics were historically over-represented in manual trades and under-represented in the North's middle class. Finally, an ingrained distrust and reluctance to participate in the governing of the state, whether in political life or in the civil service, had marked the nationalist outlook from the early 1920s. Despite these facts, however, it was the *perception* of discrimination in these specific instances that drove forward the burgeoning civil rights movement in the 1960s.[18]

In fact the movement was a culmination of the lobbying of several left- and right-wing groups, as well as individual liberals and socialists. The unifying idea was that Unionist Party malpractice had been directed towards all non-Unionists and adversely affected the working class. Thus, in May 1965, the Belfast Trade Union Congress sponsored a special meeting to discuss gerrymandering and police reform. The NILP, the Communist Party, the middle-class Campaign for Social Justice, as well as republican representatives, all attended. For the first time since the 1930s, a cross-sectarian, anti-Unionist movement abandoned nationalistic rhetoric and campaigned under the slogan, 'British rights for British citizens'.

However, the problem for many unionists was that the movement was tainted due to its links to hard-line republicans. For example, the decision to form the Northern Ireland Civil Rights Association (NICRA) was taken in August 1966 at the home of a well-known IRA man.[19] In Stormont, meanwhile, Prime Minister Terence O'Neill was coming under pressure from Harold Wilson's Labour government, which had won the 1964 general election, to end gerrymandering and reorganise the allocation of houses and local government jobs. O'Neill was forced to balance these demands with the reluctance of his right-wing political faction to be seen as giving in to extra-constitutional pressure. O'Neill's dilemma was further complicated by the emergence of a charismatic preacher who resisted attempts at conciliation. Thus, Ian Paisley famously ridiculed O'Neill's softly-softly approach by claiming that there was no difference between bridge-builders and traitors: they both cross to the other side. Although some commentators have suggested that the O'Neill premiership was a 'missed opportunity',[20] there is little to suggest that he envisaged anything more radical than economic modernisation. O'Neill's paternalistic approach to politics had little to offer the urban working classes and even less to the Catholics mobilised by the goals of civil rights.

O'Neill's reluctance to countenance radical reform influenced the decision by key civil rights leaders to import the lessons Martin Luther King had used in the US in the early 1960s. They were encouraged to move beyond the purely constitutional sphere – namely, to move from lobbying and publishing reports to street protests – by Labour Party supporters such as Paul Rose MP, who claimed that Westminster would never intervene unless forced to do so by events on the ground. Thus on 18 June 1968 Austin Currie squatted in a house in Caledon, County Tyrone, which had been allocated to a nineteen-year-old Protestant woman even though several Catholic families had been placed on the waiting list for such housing.[21] Despite some media coverage, the movement continued to struggle to gain popular support. Thus a protest march in Derry on 5 October 1968 mustered somewhere between 200 and 400 people. It was the response of the Royal Ulster Constabulary (RUC), relayed on television news across the UK and Ireland, which turned the campaign into a mass movement: the scenes of police batoning unarmed protesters inspired 15,000–20,000 people to join a reprised march the following month.

O'Neill was urgently summoned to Downing Street and, in response to the growing pressure, issued a five-point plan in November: a development commission would take over the responsibilities of the Londonderry Corporation; the Special Powers Act was to be abolished; electoral practices were to be reformed; housing allocation would be overseen by a new authority; and an ombudsman was to be appointed to deal with complaints against government. For student radicals such as Eamonn McCann and Michael Farrell this was too little, too late, and while NICRA announced a moratorium on marching, this radical faction of the movement – organised under the banner 'People's Democracy' – decided to push ahead with plans to hold a 'long march' from Belfast to Londonderry.

The People's Democracy march proceeded from Belfast to Derry at the beginning of January 1969. The route, a distance of a hundred or so miles, inevitably passed directly through unionist heartlands and the marchers were repeatedly attacked along the way by loyalist protesters. The most serious incident occurred a few miles outside Derry City, when the march was ambushed by protesters and non-uniformed B Specials, wielding rocks and sticks at Burntollet Bridge. The importance of the students' march has been underlined by one prominent historian, who claims that:

It could be argued that the march marks the pivotal point at which the Troubles changed from being primarily about civil rights to being about the more traditional disputes concerning national and religious identities.[22]

The reason for this is that the 1969 march broke the unspoken communal rule that, in Northern Ireland, marching designates ownership of an area. The marchers saw – and continue to see – themselves as part of a global human rights movement and consciously copied the mass mobilisation techniques of rallies, and peaceful protests of other radical movements across Europe and America:

the practice of discrimination has similar characteristics whether its victims live in Soweto, Watts, or North Belfast. What cannot be denied is that the move towards democracy, in Northern Ireland as elsewhere, required recognition of the abnormality of exclusion and the development of norms based on universal human rights.[23]

Martin Luther King and the black civil rights struggle, in particular, provided a model to be copied. Northern Ireland, however, was not the southern states of America, or South Africa, or Paris. In fact, Northern Ireland was a region where the state itself was (and is) contested and provoking the police would be unlikely to win allies in government as King had done.

The triggering of ethnic sentiments effectively ended the civil rights movement as national rather than political or legal issues quickly came to dominate the political agenda. The downward cycle of inter-communal confrontation continued throughout 1969, leading to the decision by Westminster to send troops on to the streets in August. Recognising an opportunity to settle the Irish question once and for all, a tiny cabal of republicans decided to 'take the war to the Brits' and initiated violent attacks against the army in 1970.

**CONSTITUTIONAL NATIONALISM: THE SOCIAL
DEMOCRATIC AND LABOUR PARTY**

The SDLP was formed in August 1970 in order to present a more
cohesive anti-unionist front at Stormont. The party's leadership
comprised socialist and nationalist politicians and civil rights veter-
ans. The party's first leader, Gerry Fitt, was replaced by his deputy
John Hume in 1979 (who was succeeded by Mark Durkan in 2001).
The party advocated a reformist nationalist position and sought to
promote broad socialistic principles.

The unravelling of the state

The disintegration of the Northern Ireland state caused
widespread consternation in British political circles. Harold
Wilson had long professed his ignorance of the circumstances
leading up to the civil rights marches of the late 1960s. However,
in keeping with earlier protocol, Wilson had been receiving
regular briefings from the NILP – British Labour's sister party in
the province – for decades, so much so that these updates
informed the latter's overall policy on Northern Ireland, as well
as its dealings with its local constituency parties.[24] By playing up
his ignorance of the conflict in the province Wilson sought to
stave off criticism from Labour backbenchers, while avoiding
political acrimony on the part of the Conservative opposition.
Despite the disconnection often emphasised in some accounts of
Labour policy and Northern Ireland, the party's annual conference in 1969 carried a motion which commended the government's handling of the situation, emphasising how conference:

> recognises the presence of the British Army as essential for the
> restoration of peace; commends the ability with which the
> Home Secretary brought all responsible leaders together during
> his visit to Northern Ireland; supports the peace formula

devised by the Home Secretary and having as its basis equality for all and reforms where injustice has been evident; and welcomes the Labour Party's consultation with both the Irish Labour Party and the NILP.[25]

THE BIRTH OF THE PROVISIONAL IRA: THE BURNING OF BOMBAY STREET AND THE FALLS CURFEW

The burning of Bombay Street, off the Catholic Falls Road, during ethnic riots in August 1969 and the curfew imposed by the British Army on the Falls in June 1970 are central to the Provisional IRA's (PIRA) narrative of the Troubles. This narrative runs as follows: Protestant pogroms such as Bombay Street, which witnessed mass evacuations of Catholics, and British Army incursions such as in the Falls area between 2 and 5 June 1970, during which five Catholics were killed, demonstrated the necessity of a defence force to take the place of the inept, unprepared, and complacent structures which had been in place until then. This new faction – the Provisional IRA – was established in *response* to Protestant and British aggression at the end of 1969, splitting away from what became known as the 'Officials' and taking a more aggressive and sectarian war to the British Army and the Protestant community than was the case previously.[26]

This self-serving justification is plausible only if the historical context is telescoped and the preceding events airbrushed out of existence. In fact, the IRA was not run down during the 1960s and recruitment was steadily rising (from 657 volunteers in 1962 to 1039 in 1966).[27] Second, the burning of Bombay Street occurred *following* two nights of IRA-inspired rioting against loyalists who, regardless of the amount of guns, were fearful of *any* guns in the hands of republicans. Third, the Falls Road curfew occurred in response to the newly formed PIRA embarking on a bombing campaign. Arguably, Protestant and British Army onslaughts might have occurred in the absence of the IRA, however, there is no getting away from the fact that its existence in Catholic areas contributed enormously to the sufferings ordinary individuals endured.[28]

British policy under the Conservative government headed by Edward Heath, which replaced Labour in June 1970, was more robust on security. A constant worry for British government officials was the adverse affect that the Northern Ireland conflict was now having on the UK's reputation abroad. In an early draft of a Foreign and Commonwealth Office briefing paper on Northern Ireland, one civil servant bemoaned how:

> No current issue of our foreign policy touches the national interest and the security of Britain more closely, or could, in the immediate future, do more damage to our international standing … Northern Ireland is not exclusively a domestic issue; we shall not escape international damage merely because we are still working out a long-term solution to a domestic problem. Our choice – and the time we take to reach it – will not merely shape our relationship with the Irish Republic: it may lastingly determine the political characteristics of that geographically inescapable neighbour. Success or failure in Ulster could mean the difference, in American eyes, between Britain as an asset and Britain as a liability. Our other foreign friends are watching us anxiously, our enemies with gloating expectation. Our great strength, which has long outweighed many weaknesses, has always been the solidarity of our nation-state. It is this which is now beginning to be threatened in Ulster.[29]

Countering such embarrassment had been the focus of British policy towards its involvement in other small wars for much of the post-war period, in places as geographically diverse as Palestine, Malaya, and Aden, in large part because of a failure to formulate a coherent non-party-specific strategy to deal with ethnic violence. Nevertheless, stabilising the security situation became a top priority for the British government in London and several avenues were explored to reduce the violence. Despite

BLOODY SUNDAY, JANUARY 1972

The shooting dead of thirteen unarmed men (a fourteenth died later) by the Parachute Regiment during an anti-internment march in Derry on 30 January 1972 remains one of the most controversial incidents of the Troubles. The shooting began following the attempt by around 100 youths to climb over a street barrier to attack the army with stones and iron bars. Although it has never been established who fired the first shot, the best account of the day indicates that the IRA were active in the area at the time and most likely opened fire on the army.[30] While Martin McGuinness, who was then in charge of the IRA in Derry, has never given a full account of his knowledge about the day, there is no doubt that the army was responsible for committing an atrocity.

The immediate context has been lost, however, amidst the historic fall-out – not least the burning of the British embassy in Dublin in the immediate aftermath and nationalists' rejection of the hastily convened Widgery Tribunal inquiry into the events, which exonerated the army and claimed that some of the victims were carrying pipe-bombs. Republicans subsequently moved to harness nationalist discontent and used it as a means of mobilising support and recruiting IRA volunteers. In 1998 New Labour established a new inquiry under Lord Saville to investigate the events. Documents released under the auspices of that inquiry reveal that there is no foundation for the republican claim that the army was trying to teach Catholics a lesson. In fact, in the weeks leading up to the march the IRA had sought to exacerbate and create a situation where the army would be confronted by or retaliate against ordinary Catholics. Thus hundreds of rounds had been fired at security forces in the first weeks of 1972, culminating in the killing of a soldier and two policemen on 27 January. A US philosopher has recently concluded that while the British Army cannot be absolved of its *direct responsibility for its actions* ... there is no reason to suppose that these events [namely, the Falls Road curfew, internment, and Bloody Sunday] *would* have happened without the prior provocations supplied by the IRA'.[31] The Bloody Sunday Inquiry has yet to publish its findings.

its self-professed role as defenders of the Catholic community and then as an offensive military response to force the end of the Stormont government and British withdrawal, the IRA remained sensitive to political realities. In early March 1972 the organisation instructed its units to 'suspend military operations for a period of seventy-two hours', although it reserved the 'right to engage in defensive action', in order to facilitate negotiations with the British government. The IRA remained resolute on three points, expressed by its spokesman in Dublin as:

1   An immediate withdrawal of British armed forces from the streets of Northern Ireland, coupled with a statement of intent as to the eventual evacuation of Her Majesty's Forces and an acknowledgement of the right of the Irish people to determine their own future without interference from the British Government
2   Abolition of the Stormont Parliament
3   A total amnesty for all political prisoners in Ireland and England, both tried and untried, and for all those on the wanted list.[32]

Now Leader of the Opposition, Harold Wilson offered the IRA an unexpected olive branch by proposing that all internees should be released, except those against whom criminal charges were preferred in courts.[33] British political elites played their part in escalating the Troubles by indulging the IRA's belief that British forces were about to withdraw. A key example of this was when Wilson, as Leader of the Opposition, held a secret meeting with the IRA in Dublin at the home of Irish Labour Party Teachta Dála (TD) (Member of the Irish Parliament) Dr John O'Connell. The meeting was the first of a number of high-level meetings that would take place between the IRA and British politicians throughout the conflict.

EXTRACT FROM THE HAROLD WILSON–IRA MEETING, DUBLIN, 13 MARCH 1972

Mr Wilson: 'On the three points, which are totally unacceptable as they stand, I would say this: the British army forces should revert to a peacekeeping role, not one of search and arrest, qualified if we do a guns ban. At the end of the day, the people of Ireland must decide if they want the British forces there. I wanted British troops to stay for a long time. Point two: there are strong suspicions that the Government want a suspension of Stormont and to replace it with a commission. If they propose that the hold would be a lot less on the Unionist side. If they propose a transfer of security responsibility that is an effective end of the Stormont Parliament. I would not like to think that the war would be continued over this argument. The third point: a total amnesty for 'political prisoners'. That means the men who committed Aldershot. No British Government could accept point three after Aldershot. I would not accept it, nor would any British Government.'

Mr A [David O'Connell]: 'Not even after Bloody Sunday?'

Mr Wilson: 'No. An amnesty comes at the end of a political settlement. Makarios, Kenyatta ... the amnesty followed the political settlement. I do not think this is out [indicating the IRA document] I would put three and two on the agenda of all-party negotiations. At the end of the day, an amnesty is on. At an appropriate point I will send a message through John O'Connell and say, 'For God's sake, give us a truce'.[34]

Once Wilson's meeting with the IRA was leaked to the press he found himself subject to heavy criticism not only from Unionists and loyalists but also from his supporters in the NILP. The proceedings of the meeting suggest that Wilson and Rees were not only politically naive – in assuming that the IRA were politically astute – but also that they underestimated the reaction of the Protestant working class. It was obvious that the British Labour Party had by now bought into the SDLP's political position. In many ways it also vindicated Unionist hostility towards the Labour Party, especially those in the NILP who rejected the link to a party whose hierarchy had moved towards a flaccid acceptance of the nationalist perspective on Northern Irish politics.[35] This was confirmed in a letter to Conor Cruise O'Brien, in which Wilson defended his entry into secret talks with the IRA.[36] Undoubtedly the Provisional IRA's position was coloured by the need to explore the possibility of British withdrawal. Nonetheless, as Leader of the Opposition, Wilson was not in a position to facilitate the IRA's demands. Newspaper speculation even suggested that the organisation was undergoing a radical restructuring, in large part because of the death or capture of over a dozen personnel, several in key positions, in the space of a ten-week period in the spring of 1972. Added to the heavy casualty rate was the unstable nature of its explosive stockpiles and the upsurge in 'own goals'.[37] The IRA sought to develop itself as

RADICAL UNIONISM: THE DEMOCRATIC UNIONIST PARTY

The DUP was formed in September 1971 by the Revd Ian Paisley and Desmond Boal, following their unsuccessful attempt to entice William Craig and others in the Unionist Party's right wing to form a new party. Boal said that the party's position would be 'on the right on constitutional issues and on the left on social issues'. The party drew support initially from Paisley's Free Presbyterian Church and evangelical Protestants. Vigorously opposed to accommodative tendencies within the Unionist Party – such as power sharing and cross-border cooperation – the DUP eventually overtook the latter as the main representative of Ulster unionism in 2003, and in May 2007 agreed to share power with republicans and work in the north–south bodies instituted under the Belfast/Good Friday Agreement. The party was led by Paisley from its inception until May 2008 when he was succeeded by Peter Robinson.

a professional organisation in the early 1970s, extending its bombing campaign to mainland Britain in 1974 to alleviate the pressure on its embattled volunteers in Northern Ireland.

The end of majority rule

Despite Wilson's interference, the British policy of bi-partisanship on Northern Ireland affairs remained the norm in the House of Commons. It was not until 1974 that the Labour Party would be in a position to influence government policy on the province. By 1971–2 it was also clear that the Unionist government had now lost support from a significant proportion of the Protestant population; many grass-roots loyalists deserted them in favour of the newly formed Democratic Unionist Party (DUP) or loyalist paramilitary organisations. Hemmed in on one side by an indignant minority nationalist community, which desired not only the abolition of Stormont but also a greater share in the province's future, and on the other by a British government impervious to Unionist reassurances that the security situation was under control, the local regime had little wriggle room. What made the decision-making process more difficult was the double-sided effects of an escalation of the violent conflict by armed groupings on both sides and the increasing loss of control over the situation by the local security forces.

Events came to a head when Prime Minister Edward Heath signed an order discontinuing the Stormont Parliament on 24 March 1972, thus bringing down the final curtain on fifty years of Unionist dominance in the region. Almost immediately it 'reduced overnight the Unionist Party from a party of government with patronage at its disposal, to a body of incoherent and ineffectual protest'.[38] Now that the death-knell had to all intents and purposes been sounded on the local parliament, a disgruntled Heath and his newly installed Secretary of State for

Northern Ireland, William Whitelaw, set out on an arbitration process to coax the local parties towards finding an accommodation acceptable to both sides of the divided community. In his political memoirs, the last Unionist Prime Minister Brian Faulkner lamented how the prorogation had occurred without prior consultation with either him or his cabinet. Faulkner railed against direct rule and was particularly disdainful of the 'coconut commission' of advisors on whom Whitelaw depended, attempting to organise a campaign for the reinstatement of Stormont.[39]

The effects of the fall of Stormont were far-reaching. For the Unionist Party's principal base of support, the Protestant working class, it spelt social and political disaster. While far from enjoying a privileged position, this social grouping did constitute the largest and most loyal section of society and was ultimately the popular support-base upon which Unionist power rested. It was now in danger of fragmenting.[40]

Conclusion

The birth of the Northern Ireland state had taken place in the wake of a devastating total war, and it was to break down in the chaos of intra-state civil disturbance, armed insurgency, and violent reprisals. Thus, Northern Ireland did not escape from the radicalisation which had thrown up rival ethnic, national, and religious groups in other parts of Europe, nor would it escape unscathed from the dire effects of exclusionary ethnic violence. In 1920–2, between 452 and 463 people had been killed by inter-communal violence; almost the same number of people died in 1972 alone. The fear of a resurgent IRA led to the pre-emptive re-emergence of militant loyalism in the form of the UVF in 1965–6. While it was initially a short-lived affair (the RUC arrested many of its leading lights) the organisation remained in existence, occasionally participating in selected bombing missions that forced Terence O'Neill from office. Moreover, the IRA split, internment, and Bloody Sunday all acted collectively as a recruiting mechanism for a more militant IRA defenderism in the form of the Provisional IRA. Ulster stood at the crossroads.

2

Direct rule and power sharing, 1972–4

Britain intervenes: the imposition of direct rule from London

The year 1972 was the bloodiest in the history of the Northern Ireland Troubles, with both republican and loyalist terrorists embarking on a radical escalation of their violent campaigns. In total, 497 people died. The month of July alone witnessed nearly a hundred deaths. Over 10,000 shooting incidents and over 1300 car bombings occurred during the course of the year. Horrific massacres left blood-soaked memories in the fabric of society, including Bloody Sunday (30 January), when British soldiers from the 1st Battalion Parachute Regiment opened fire on a civil rights march in Derry City killing fourteen people. The Official IRA retaliated some weeks later with a car bombing of the Parachute Regiment's Aldershot headquarters, which killed seven soldiers. The bloodshed continued in the form of individual assassinations and stand-out atrocities such as Bloody Friday (21 July), when the PIRA planted twenty-two bombs around Belfast, killing nine and injuring 130, and the PIRA bombing of the village of Claudy (31 July), which left nine people dead.

Individual acts of carnage also horrified many people: for example, the execution of the nineteen-year-old Royal Irish Rangers soldier William Best, a Catholic, who was at home on leave in Derry, sparked a protest from over 200 local women at the Official Republican headquarters in the city and shamed the movement into abandoning its armed campaign. Elsewhere, the sectarian killing of the fourteen-year-old schoolboy David McClenaghan in North Belfast on 11 July was described by the judge in the ensuing trial as the worst crime ever to come before the courts, representing 'the lowest level of human depravity'. The boy, who was mentally handicapped, was shot dead when four men linked to the Ulster Defence Association (UDA) and UVF broke into his home and raped his mother.

Amidst this spiralling violence and the resulting communal tensions, the British government introduced direct rule from London with the greatest reluctance and with no long-term, coherent, or strategic vision for the political vacuum it created. Indeed, the lack of certainty in British political circles simply fuelled the suspicions of the paramilitaries and the local political parties – all of whom simply read their own fears and/or ambitions into the government's ambiguities. For example, although the army deployed heavy-handed tactics at certain times, the apparent willingness of Westminster politicians to enter into dialogue with the IRA fuelled unionist fears of an imminent British withdrawal. Unionist responses split between populist anger – expressed by politicians such as Ian Paisley or William Craig – and the attempt by the Unionist Party leader, Brian Faulkner, to try to manage the pace of change by negotiating with the Conservative government. On the other hand, nationalists perceived the changed political context as having opened up new opportunities for progress and the SDLP sought to pocket perceived gains and build towards gradual reunification. For the IRA, the introduction of direct rule was a major victory – as the organisation's then officer commanding (OC) in Derry, Martin McGuinness, remarked at the time how 'people are going around seeking for peace [sic]. They are wasting their time. We are fighting on. We are not stopping until we get a united Ireland.'[1]

LOYALIST VIGILANTISM: THE UDA

The Ulster Defence Association emerged in response to the IRA's armed offensive in 1971. Founded in the summer of 1971 the UDA brought together former trade unionists, soldiers, and members of local communities across Northern Ireland. It was responsible for approximately 259 deaths in the conflict, despite remaining a legal organisation until 1992. Throughout the Troubles it claimed responsibility for its terrorist acts through the Ulster Freedom Fighters, a *nom de guerre*. The UDA called a halt to its armed campaign in November 2007 and decommissioned its weaponry in June 2009. Although it had split with its faction in south-east Antrim in 2006, the latter announced that it was working towards a conflict transformation endgame which would result in its full disarmament.

Having taken the decision to assume control of the province, Prime Minister Edward Heath therefore found himself faced with a complicated dilemma that was to confront successive British governments. First, given the disparate ideological viewpoints and the divergent assessments of political change, Britain's capacity to improve the situation was extremely limited. Second, any attempts to introduce radical policies would, as Heath would shortly discover, most likely meet with resistance from either nationalists or unionists (or both). Third, choosing to do nothing was also fraught with difficulty – for even in avoiding political initiatives, the British government inspired constant complaints of favouritism or supporting the status quo by nationalists, or of capitulation and speculation about its real intentions by unionists. In short, while the assumption of direct rule by London was intended to manage the deepening political stalemate, British state intervention in Northern Ireland had the unintended consequence of contributing to the further entrenchment of the North's divided politics.

Recognising these limitations, British officials hoped that direct rule would be a stop-gap solution. However, for much of the next thirty-five years the running of the country was chiefly the concern of the Secretary of State for Northern Ireland, who was assisted by junior ministers and advised by the Northern Ireland Office (NIO). Heath installed the then Leader of the House of Commons William Whitelaw as the first Secretary of State. Although Whitelaw was instrumental in securing the agreement to set up a power-sharing executive in 1973, his initial dealings with republicans caused widespread consternation. For example, in June 1972, following a series of preliminary and confidential meetings with the SDLP, and in response to a hunger strike by republican prisoners in Crumlin Road Gaol, Whitelaw conceded 'special category status', allowing more visits and the use of civilian clothes for paramilitary prisoners. In certain respects that decision was the time bomb that would eventually lead to the hunger strikes in the early 1980s – in which republican prisoners rejected attempts to treat them as ordinary criminals. Certainly, the republican delegation thought so. Having been flown to the London home of NIO Minister Paul Channon, the PIRA delegation – which included Séamus Twomey, Seán MacStiofáin, Ivor Bell, Dáithí Ó Conaill, a young Gerry Adams (released from prison especially for the occasion), and Martin McGuinness – had little intention of negotiating and simply demanded that the British withdraw from the North by the end of 1975. Whitelaw later wrote:

> The meeting was a non-event. The IRA leaders simply made impossible demands which I told them the British government would never concede. They were in fact still in a mood of defiance and determination to carry on until their absurd ultimatums were met.[2]

Having called a truce in order to facilitate the meeting, the Provisionals quickly returned to full-scale operations by killing three soldiers and a civilian on 13 July. In response to the renewed violence and the killings on Bloody Friday, Whitelaw ordered the army to enter those areas of Belfast and Derry that had been barricaded off and occupied by the IRA. Involving 12,000 troops, Operation Motorman (31 July) was the largest British military operation since the Suez Canal Crisis of 1956. The operation passed off relatively peacefully in the urban areas, but coincided with the PIRA's bombing of Claudy. Whitelaw next turned to the elected representatives and invited the main political parties to a conference in September in an effort to try to kick-start talks and break the impasse. Nonetheless, regardless of the ideological gulf separating the politicians, the ongoing issue of internment meant that the SDLP was reluctant to enter into dialogue, while the resurgent IRA campaign and the fall-out from the imposition of direct rule hindered the prospects of unionist politicians being open to compromise.

Responses to direct rule

The assumption of direct rule from London ended the dominant position enjoyed for half a century by the Ulster Unionist Party as the party of government in Northern Ireland. Furthermore, since Westminster was committed to giving Catholics a greater say in the running of the North, this effectively meant that the UUP could only hope to maintain the Union by negotiating with the SDLP – even those well disposed to trying to reach an accommodation with Westminster, such as Brian Faulkner, baulked at the prospect. Thus, while the 'Irish dimension' – namely, the idea of giving Dublin a greater say in Northern affairs – posed a massive problem for unionists, it is a common mistake to overemphasise the issue to the detriment of concerns created by the prospect of power sharing. Giving nationalists a stake in the running of a country which they traditionally regarded as a failed entity was incongruent for many unionists; for while they accepted the principle of power sharing, serious reservations persisted regarding which party power would be shared with and at what level. Thus, although Brian Faulkner had agreed to recognise Dublin having a greater role in Northern Ireland in 1971, he continued to resist executive power sharing during 1972 and much of 1973. For example, at the beginning of 1973, he warned that:

> I find it hard to conceive how any government in Ulster could hope to operate effectively were any substantial power to obstruct its operations placed in the hands of such men. There are those at Westminster who would advocate just such an arrangement by building in sectarian representation to the executive of the new Stormont Assembly. To do so would be to court disaster and make Ulster ungovernable.[3]

In part, Faulkner was simply expressing embedded unionist distrust of the intentions of nationalist politicians. Linked with this was the fact that many unionists believed that the new nationalist leadership, the SDLP, had risen to prominence on the back of republican violence and saw key leaders such as Gerry Fitt, John Hume, and Austin Currie as being instrumental in the civil rights campaign of the 1960s that had done so much to undermine and destabilise the Northern state. In addition, Faulkner was also concerned with the fact that if the SDLP were to be awarded seats in any new Northern Ireland executive, then a similar provision might also have to be made for his intra-bloc opponents: Ian Paisley and Bill Craig.

While the changed political circumstances presented new challenges for Faulkner's Unionist Party, they opened up new opportunities for Irish nationalists, and the SDLP, in particular, recognised and sought to take advantage of these changes. Far from simply reacting to the pressures of being 'out-nationalised'

BRIAN FAULKNER

Brian Faulkner has become the totemic unionist figure who represents the dangers of leaders moving too far ahead of their grass roots in the search for political accommodation. Faulkner's political career ended in a series of disastrous elections following his failed attempt to operate a power-sharing administration with the SDLP and his decision to countenance a Council of Ireland. Subsequent unionist leaders such as William Craig in 1975 or, more recently, David Trimble in 2005, have been criticised for not being savvy enough to heed the warning from history regarding moderation. Yet, Faulkner's move to accommodative politics occurred very gradually and in fact he only agreed to share power and acquiesce in the Council of Ireland once he was certain that his majority in the Northern Ireland Assembly would be reflected in the Northern Ireland executive and be awarded veto rights over the Council.

Faulkner rose to power in the Unionist Party due to his business reputation and he railed against the 'Big House', aristocratic tendencies of the unionist elites. His early political career was based on his opposition to the reformist premiership of Terence O'Neill (1963–9). He had previously provoked nationalist animosity during his time as Minister of Home Affairs when he pushed Orange marches through the Catholic village of Dungiven in 1959.[4] When Faulkner was appointed Leader of the Unionist Party and Prime Minister of Northern Ireland in March 1971, he moved to try to stem the growing tide of communal division. His offer of committee seats to the SDLP in June 1971 was, however, quickly overtaken by events – the SDLP withdrew from Stormont a couple of weeks later in protest against the army killing two Catholics in Derry. Furthermore, he introduced internment in August provoking widespread nationalist protest and leaving many in the SDLP with bitter memories regarding Faulkner himself. Indeed, the comment by one of his political opponents, Lindsay Kennedy, is representative of how he was seen by many at the time within unionism: 'He has a lust for office, is cunning, and has no imagination.'[5] In the light of the subsequent persistence of the conflict, commentators have often offered a more benign assessment of Faulkner based on the idea that his initiatives in 1973–4 represented something of a missed opportunity. Faulkner died in a hunting accident in 1977.

by the republican movement, it followed a nationalistic course of its own that became more pronounced after the Provisionals' failure to win concrete concessions from Whitelaw in the summer of 1972. It attempted to capture the political initiative after the killing of Ranger Best in May as party leaders, such as John Hume and Ivan Cooper, rejected any accusations of 'selling-out' the internees by entertaining hopes of political dialogue. Instead, they questioned the motivation behind the republicans' campaign by claiming that it was PIRA violence – rather than political or civil repression – that was keeping the internees imprisoned. Cooper, in particular, sought to break out of the straitjacket of disengagement by warning that Northern Ireland was in danger of being overtaken by a 'lunatic fringe' and that flexibility was needed to tackle sectarianism.[6]

The party continued to complain to both Heath and Whitelaw during the summer of 1972 over internment. Though, as one of the party founders, Paddy Devlin, later pointed out, the SDLP utilised the issue in order to claim a certain moral authority and as a means of leveraging other political gain from Westminster:

> Strong as our objection to internment was, it really served as an excuse for us to remain on the political high ground. We felt that we held the whip-hand in the situation and that by holding out we could minimise the concessions we would have to make and maximise the gains.[7]

The SDLP's leadership met in Bunbeg, County Donegal, at the end of August to discuss its submission to Whitelaw's conference, and while it refused to attend due to internment, it did publish a position paper – *Towards a New Ireland*. The paper called on Westminster to declare its support for a united Ireland, and, in the meantime, to establish an 'interim system of government' for Northern Ireland. This would consist of an eighty-four-member assembly elected by proportional representation and led by two appointed commissioners. Again, the paper called for Northern Ireland to be policed by the security forces of both the Republic and the UK. Furthermore, the document proposed the creation of a national senate to 'plan the integration of the whole island by preparing the harmonisation of the structures, laws and services … and to agree on a constitution'.[8] Although the power-sharing and cross-border elements of the paper would later resurface in radically transformed versions in the Sunningdale communiqué, that coincidence was more the product of British proposals than the strength of the SDLP's ideas.

Indeed, the *New Ireland* paper contained little that was attractive to unionists who, in fact, barely figured in the party's calculations. Likewise, the document was only minimally acceptable to the Lynch government in Dublin. As officials warned Lynch, the party's ideas for a national senate and quasi-joint authority would entail significant constitutional problems for the South. However, the officials advised, the SDLP's vision regarding gradual reunification was amenable to Dublin and the document gave 'considerable support to the idea that the Irish government has a *right* to be consulted by Britain'.[9]

The road to Sunningdale

In October 1972 and March 1973, the British government published two policy papers that effectively set the parameters for future talks. In particular, the March 1973 White Paper established that British government policy would be based on the need for a cross-communal (power-sharing) executive and for the Dublin government to be given some kind of formal recognition in the running of Northern Ireland (the Irish dimension). The Westminster legislation provided for a new seventy-eight-seat consultative assembly to replace Stormont and to be elected by proportional representation. Quite how those ideas were to be fleshed out remained a matter of speculation and feverish political manoeuvring.

Although Dublin officials were reticent about publicly supporting the SDLP's *Towards a New Ireland* paper, they quickly developed detailed plans regarding cross-border bodies. Taking their cue from the SDLP's document and the October 1972 White Paper, Southern officials proceeded from the premise that a 'meaningful North–South link' would form part of an 'interim solution', which would be 'sufficiently dynamic and evolutionary to create a climate which ultimately might lead to Irish unity'.[10] In order to facilitate this 'dynamic', officials envisaged a two-tier 'Council of Ireland' with consultative (parliamentary) and executive (ministerial) levels. The potential obstacle of unionist resistance or, in nationalist-speak, 'intransigence' could be surmounted or bypassed through what officials called the 'momentum towards eventual political unity'. In short, economic and security harmonisation would create a political climate in which reunification was a small, logical, and unavoidable step.

This mode of thinking carried over during the change of government in March 1973, when Jack Lynch's Fianna Fáil party was replaced by a Fine Gael–Labour coalition led by Liam Cosgrave. Although the coalition's decision to pursue a nationalist agenda may have been influenced by the fact that it was in power due to a one-seat margin over the traditionally more nationalistic Fianna Fáil, in fact even behind the scenes, the government did not take unionist fears seriously – state papers reveal that the views of the cabinet's most sceptical minister, Conor Cruise O'Brien, were largely frozen out of deliberations. Instead, the Department of Foreign Affairs, headed by Garret FitzGerald (himself a close friend and confidant of John Hume), drove forward government policymaking. The tenor of that policymaking is demonstrated in the initial drafts for the

Council of Ireland of May 1973, which gained cabinet approval in June. These plans claim that Dublin should be 'in no way committed to the agenda set out in the [British] White Paper'. Instead, Dublin should pursue a 'strong Council of Ireland with real functions to perform'. The Council should be both executive and evolutionary – 'an embryo and symbol of our working towards unity based on consent'.[11]

Despite the inclusion of the principle of consent, the editorial of the unionist daily, the *Newsletter*, drew little comfort:

> It is a case of 'heads I win; tails you lose'. What we are being offered, in effect, is a one-way ticket to Dublin, the only question outstanding – the date on which we are to be coerced into using it.[12]

Backed by the Dublin government, the SDLP sought to maximise its gains and looked to yield little ground to Faulkner as regards the Council of Ireland. The party had won nineteen of the newly established Northern Ireland Assembly's seventy-eight seats in June 1973 and attempted to make the most of an ascendant position. Thus, while Whitelaw was trying to engineer talks on power sharing, the SDLP sought to capitalise on intra-unionist discontent and pushed for a strong Irish dimension, even if it meant forgoing agreement on executive power sharing within Northern Ireland. In September John Hume told the Irish government that:

> Now that Faulkner was at his weakest … it [was] more important than ever that he should be inextricably tied to a fully worked out and agreed Council before the executive was formally established.[13]

The SDLP were suspicious that if a power-sharing executive was agreed prior to the cross-border institutions Faulkner would stall the process and become more difficult.

JOHN HUME

In many ways, the quintessential example of the thesis that the civil rights movement was a product of a growing and aspirational Catholic middle class – a civil rights leader and a founding member of the Credit Union movement in Ireland – John Hume placed himself at the centre of modern Irish nationalism. And despite the whiff-of-cordite attraction that Gerry Adams seemingly exerts on many commentators, Hume remains the key figure in nationalist politics in the second half of the twentieth century.

A keen student of history – he holds a Master's from Maynooth College – Hume frequently cited the nineteenth-century Home Rule leader, Charles Stewart Parnell, as his political guru. The Parnell figure in Hume's imagery, however, is not the Joycean rebel against provincial Catholic morality (Parnell's political career ended following a highly publicised affair)[14] – rather, it is the Parnell who fought against unionist intransigence, who struggled to convince a reluctant British government of the worth of his vision, and who sought to hold back the primordial violence threatened by hard-line republicans.[15] He quoted Parnell during his talks with Gerry Adams in 1988: 'Ireland can never [be] united and can never be free until the prejudices of the Protestant people are conciliated.' The Parnell imagery is also apt in that, like Parnell, Hume underestimated the strength of unionist opposition to an all-Ireland state. As his political biographer points out, 'Hume's greatest failure was his inability to engage at an intellectual level with unionist arguments.'[16] This occurred not only in his willingness to entertain Adams from 1988 onwards – to the dismay of many within the SDLP – but was evident from the early 1970s, as revealed in his advice to the Dublin government to tie Faulkner into a strong Council of Ireland.

A counter-argument can be made, however, that Hume's ideas (already developed as early as 1972) underpinned the 1998 Agreement – namely, the desirability of power sharing within Northern Ireland and the need for North–South cooperation in order to recognise nationalists' identities and legitimate aspirations. In this view, the Parnellite imagery is even more forceful – Hume achieved (or at least set the foundations for) something that Parnell was prevented from reaching: namely, nationalist and unionist agreement. Hume was awarded the Nobel Peace Prize together with the then UUP leader, David Trimble, in 1998.

For the SDLP, Brian Faulkner was a hate-figure who introduced internment. However, he was the only major unionist
figure with whom they could deal since the extreme right,
consisting of Paisley and Craig and their respective supporters in
the DUP and Vanguard parties, were adamantly opposed to
sharing executive power with nationalists. To compound
matters, Faulkner had serious party problems of his own. He had
entered the Assembly elections with a party that was severely
divided over how to respond to the government's White Paper.
In a desperate effort to keep his party together, Faulkner had
asked all Unionist Party candidates to sign a pledge:

> We are not opposed to power sharing in government, but we
> will not be prepared to participate in government with those
> whose *primary aim* is to break the Union with Great Britain.
> (emphasis added)[17]

The outcome of the election saw the 'Official' Unionists winning
twenty-four of the Assembly's seventy-eight seats, while the
dissident, 'Unpledged' faction won eight. Although the Unionist
Party did not formally split until the following year, the anti-
White Paper faction were already much closer in policy terms to
the DUP and Vanguard parties, and the West Belfast Loyalist
independents, who won eight, seven, and three seats respectively.
The remaining seats were won by the pro-White Paper groupings, the NILP (one), and the bi-confessional (that is, drawing
votes from across the religious divide) Alliance Party (eight).
Faulkner's numbers were further depleted following the death in
a car accident of one of his Assembly Members, David
McCarthy, while another, Nat Minford, was elected Speaker. A
further two of his faction, Austin Ardill and Jim Kilfedder, were
opposed to the White Paper, although one from the anti-White
Paper faction, Leslie Morrell, crossed to the Faulkner 'side'. In
short, Faulkner could count on twenty-one votes while the anti-
White-Paper Unionists had twenty-seven.

THE POLITICAL INSTITUTIONS OF THE FIRST PEACE PROCESS (1973–4)

1   The Northern Ireland Assembly: the March 1973 Westminster White Paper called for a return of political power to Northern Ireland, which would take the form of a devolved Assembly elected by proportional representation.

2   The power-sharing executive: the Assembly would be run by an executive, which would be appointed by the Secretary of State and would command 'widespread support' across Northern Ireland. The executive would take charge of the governmental responsibilities transferred from London by the Secretary of State.

3   The Council of Ireland: the White Paper also envisaged what it termed an 'Irish dimension' – namely, bodies overseeing cross-border cooperation in socio-economic areas such as tourism, regional development, and transport. The Council of Ireland was fleshed out at the Sunningdale talks (December 1973) and was to have two tiers – a parliamentary tier to discuss pertinent issues, and a ministerial tier, consisting of ministers from the Irish Parliament, the Dáil, in Dublin and the Assembly in Belfast, which would enact policies and over which both Dublin and Belfast held vetoes. Whereas Faulkner held the Council to be what he called a 'necessary nonsense' to keep nationalists involved with the devolved Assembly, the SDLP saw it as an evolutionary body which would create a momentum towards eventual reunification.

Despite these difficulties Faulkner entered talks with the SDLP and the Alliance to try to form an executive in October. Following detailed negotiations, in which the SDLP unsuccessfully pushed for an equal number of seats, Faulkner secured a Unionist veto and a Unionist majority. As agreed on 22 November, the new power-sharing executive was to consist of eleven voting members – six Unionists, four SDLP, and one

Alliance – plus four non-voting members – two SDLP, one Unionist, and one Alliance. Faulkner secured this agreement, having won a narrow victory in the Unionist Party's main decision-making body, the Ulster Unionist Council Standing Committee, the previous day by 379 votes to 369. However, far from being a ringing endorsement of power sharing or inter-communal rapprochement, in fact Unionists remained deeply suspicious of the SDLP and the Irish government. Crucially, Faulkner had won by promising a Unionist executive majority coupled with the coercive threat that if a shared executive were to be rejected then Heath would impose a settlement on Northern Ireland.[18] Despite Faulkner's victory, the *Newsletter* queried whether the ultimate objective was power sharing or a united Ireland and pointed out that:

> One of the major weaknesses of the new Executive is that the public has formed its own opinion on the men who will serve on it. This is particularly the case in respect of the SDLP team which is associated in the minds of many people with the origins of the troubled period that began five years ago.[19]

However, Faulkner's options had narrowed considerably by the autumn of 1973. Regardless of the mounting Unionist unease with the prospect of power sharing and the Council of Ireland, he pushed the White Paper agenda forward. As he later explained:

> There was much talk of 'negotiating' further with Mr Whitelaw, but as far as I could see the die was cast and the post-White Paper situation was a completely new one.[20]

Having committed himself to accommodating the British government, Faulkner's choices were severely limited in terms of how far he could resist the efforts of the SDLP and Dublin to capitalise on the White Paper's vagueness concerning power sharing and the Irish dimension. In addition, his options were further constrained by the fact that his unionist opponents had taken up alternative positions and, as the implications of the White Paper agenda became more and more apparent, their rhetoric was beginning successfully to tap into embedded Protestant fears. For example, the *Newsletter* repeatedly claimed that political change had been favouring nationalists for at least five years – an argument that Paisley and Craig had been heavily emphasising since late 1971. Although many Unionists offered a residual loyalty to the Unionist Party after March 1972, by the summer of 1973 the party had been split in two and Paisley and Craig were joined by the leader of the Unpledged Unionists, Harry West, as part of a increasingly close anti-White-Paper coalition. As power sharing bedded in, and the Council of Ireland blueprints became public, these erstwhile rivals placed their alliance on a more formal footing and launched the United Ulster Unionist Council (UUUC) at the beginning of December.

Meanwhile, the two governments, plus delegations from the Faulknerite Unionists, the SDLP, and the Alliance Party, met at the civil service training college at Sunningdale in Berkshire between 6 and 10 December to discuss the formation of the Council of Ireland. Edward Heath was a key player in the negotiations, with Whitelaw having been replaced only recently as Secretary of State by Francis Pym. Following intense negotiations, it was agreed that the Council would consist of fourteen ministers (seven from the North, and seven from the South), a consultative body (thirty members from the Assembly and thirty from the Dáil), plus a permanent secretariat. It is important to note that the proposals would only be ratified once the Council was up and running. Although the Council was given an institutional shape, its specific areas of executive authority, its functions and responsibilities, remained outstanding and were to be agreed following discussions between the Belfast executive and the Dublin cabinet.

THE SUNNINGDALE COMMUNIQUÉ

Status declarations

The Irish and British governments issued separate declarations. The British pledged to uphold the present status of Northern Ireland for as long as the majority of its citizens desired. The Irish government meanwhile echoed these sentiments, claiming that it 'fully accepted and solemnly declared that there could be no change in the status of Northern Ireland until a majority of the people of Northern Ireland desired a change in that status'. The Irish government, however, made no mention of Articles 2 and 3 in its constitution, which claimed ownership over Northern Ireland.

Responsibilities

The Council of Ireland was to have executive powers in the following areas:
1 exploitation, conservation, and development of natural resources and the environment;
2 agricultural matters (including agricultural research, animal health, and operational aspects of the Common Agriculture Policy), forestry and fisheries;
3 cooperative ventures in the fields of trade and industry;
4 electricity generation;
5 tourism;
6 roads and transport;
7 advisory services in the field of public health;
8 sport, culture, and the arts.

The question as to why Faulkner conceded so much at Sunningdale has always troubled historians. One explanation put forward is that while the SDLP enjoyed close cooperation with the Dublin government, the Unionist delegation consisted of relatively inexperienced negotiators and came to the conference under-prepared. Certainly this has a ring of truth to it and is supported by the historical evidence. Thus, Faulkner's 'top secret' meeting with Dublin officials had, apparently, remained undisclosed as one of his colleagues, Basil McIvor, later pointed out that a central aim was to resist an executive role for the Council. McIvor also highlighted the fact that the Unionists also failed to secure their secondary objective – an extradition agreement with the South to counteract the fact that IRA volunteers sought refuge in the Republic safe in the knowledge that were they to be tried they could enter a plea of being political prisoners.[21] A related argument can be made that, by overemphasising the necessity of gaining a promise from Heath to restore policing powers at Sunningdale, Faulkner inadvertently allowed Dublin and the SDLP to exert more pressure to push for a strong Council of Ireland.[22]

In retrospect, however, there remains a considerable consistency to his journey from September 1971 to November–December 1973. That is to say, Faulkner's performance at Sunningdale cannot be divorced from his decisions over the previous two years in which he had conceded the necessity of cross-border cooperation and of accommodating Westminster. The former decision placed the Council of Ireland on the negotiating table, while the latter led directly to including an executive role for Nationalists in a power-sharing government – executive power sharing. Faulkner believed that, given the British economic support for Northern Ireland, unilateral independence was impossible; however, he had proceeded from the position that Unionist unity or a Unionist veto would be sufficient to counteract British demands. It was this belief that convinced him to countenance both power sharing and the Irish dimension. In his *Memoirs* Faulkner complained that he had been outmanoeuvred by the incremental approach of the Nationalists.[23] However, the weaknesses in his basic allocation of priorities was apparent at the time. Thus, despite his faith in the Unionist veto and the principle of consent, the *Newsletter* asked

the simple question about the need for such a body when neigh-
bouring governments should be cooperating against terrorism in
any event.[24]

The power-sharing executive, January–May 1974

The new power-sharing executive assumed office on 1 January
1974. Faulkner was Chief Executive, while Gerry Fitt, the
leader of the SDLP, took on the sinecure position as his
Deputy. Tensions over its political future were already
running high, following Liam Cosgrave's apparent repudiation
of the communiqué (in which he stated that he would not
change the constitutional claim over the North), and the fact
that a special UUUC meeting was scheduled for 4 January to
discuss and vote on whether to accept the idea of the
Council of Ireland. Faulkner apparently believed that the veto
safeguards would carry him through; however, he lost the vote
427 to 374 and resigned as party leader (remaining as leader of
the Unionist Assembly Party). His advisor, Peter McLachlan,
told Irish officials that in fact the meeting had 'been much
worse' than was reported and that Faulkner had lost the support
of most of the 'middle ground'.[25] In addition, the executive
possessed few real economic powers and no security responsibilities, meaning that its ability to influence events was severely
curtailed.

The executive's standing was further undermined by the
court case pursued in the South by Kevin Boland, TD, to the
effect that the communiqué was unconstitutional. The judgement backed Cosgrave's interpretation and ruled that in fact the
'status declaration' did not impinge on the Irish Constitution,
but that it was merely aspirational rather than a legal requirement. This judgement, coupled with the fact that the Dublin

government could not comment while the case was ongoing, did little to bolster Faulkner's standing in the eyes of the Unionist community. Rather, they effectively demolished one of his 'safeguards' and undermined his whole interpretation of the political changes taking place.

Given Faulkner's difficulties, the SDLP believed that he would begin to renege or at least stall on his commitments. The party's response was to ignore the UUUC vote and rather to push harder for ratification of the Council of Ireland. The SDLP itself was also facing backbench pressure surrounding its failure to achieve the ending of internment – evidenced by the formation of an anti-internment pressure group at the end of January. This was the wider context in which the SDLP backbencher, Hugh Logue, made his much-quoted response to a republican heckler that the Council of Ireland would 'trundle Unionists into a united Ireland'. The statement soon took on a life of its own when, following Edward Heath's shock announcement of a February general election, it was echoed in the UUUC's campaign slogan: 'Dublin is only a Sunningdale away'. The executive's demonstrable divisions, the gradual heightening of fears over power sharing and the Irish dimension, and the future direction the Sunningdale experiment was pointing in all contributed to the UUUC's landslide victory in which it won eleven of the twelve Northern Ireland Westminster seats (the SDLP leader, Gerry Fitt, held on to his West Belfast constituency). The result was a collective catastrophe for the Sunningdale experiment and a personal disaster for Faulkner, who had banked on retaining the leadership of Unionism through the auspices of the Assembly. Instead, that mantle passed to the tripartite leadership of the UUUC – Paisley, Craig, and West – who quickly set out their demands:

1   Northern Ireland representation at Westminster to be increased;

2   a restored, regional parliament, with unfettered control over security; and
3   the immediate scrapping of the Sunningdale communiqué.

Heath's electoral gamble failed to pay off when Labour was returned to power under Harold Wilson, who appointed Merlyn Rees to the post of Secretary of State for Northern Ireland. During their first meeting, Faulkner admitted that the election result had left the executive 'shattered' over the 'extent of feeling against a Council of Ireland' and the way in which 'moderate opinion ... had gone over to the loyalists'. Nevertheless, he still held out hope that, with movement from the SDLP and Dublin, Sunningdale could be saved.[26] He began to press for a phased introduction of the Council, which would see it beginning as a consultative body that would only take on executive functions following a period of confidence-building.

Rees and Labour, however, remained sceptical. The secret briefing for the meeting reveals something of the British disposition to Faulkner in particular and the Sunningdale experiment in general.[27] The papers describe Faulkner as having 'tried to overcome his natural reserve and forge links with his backbenchers'; however, the result of his efforts was to leave him politically isolated and 'very far ahead of his Assembly supporters let alone Unionist opinion'. The papers conclude that the only chance of the Sunningdale experiment surviving depended on 'a clear demonstration of greater Irish interest in improved cross-border security'. That London did not share Faulkner's vision is indicated in a letter Rees sent to Wilson following the meeting in which he warned the prime minister about the necessity of avoiding 'being faced with a crisis which hits us unexpectedly'.[28] As a result of these deliberations a top secret task force, consisting of senior cabinet ministers and high-ranking civil servants, was set up to make contingency plans in order to take back control of the day-to-day running of the North's administrative machinery.

The Dublin government was also getting cold feet, as demonstrated in a twenty-five-page memorandum drawn up in the immediate aftermath of the election.[29] For Dublin officials, Faulkner no longer commanded the same 'moral authority' as he did prior to the election, and, as a result, ratification of the communiqué was no longer a certainty. The report considered abandoning the whole experiment, but claimed that such a course would only serve to alienate the Unionists and the British, and subject Ireland to international approbation. Instead, it concluded that Sunningdale was the best option on the table but that the only way to save the experiment was through phased implementation. This option was not the preferred choice of the SDLP, however, who favoured immediate ratification and feared losing out on their main priority, the Council of Ireland, through Faulkner's weaknesses. Paddy Devlin, for example, told the Irish government that the 'loyalists should be presented with a fait accompli' and a speedy establishment of the Council in its entirety.[30]

With the division over ratification between the SDLP and the Faulknerite Unionists reaching a tipping point, events intervened to keep the executive in business. The trigger for the Ulster Workers' Council (UWC) strike was the defeat of a UUUC assembly motion condemning power sharing and the Council of Ireland on 14 May. In the press room of the Parliament Buildings at Stormont, Bob Pagels and Harry Murray of the UWC informed journalists that a general strike would begin immediately, with electricity output reduced from 725 to 400 megawatts. Until that point the UWC had been an almost completely unknown entity and the strike itself surprised many of even the most sharp-sighted political commentators. The UWC leadership consisted of politicians, including Paisley, Craig, and West, together with loyalist paramilitary leaders such as Andy Tyrie of the UDA, Glen Barr of the UDA (who was also an Assembly Member), and Ken Gibson of the UVF. The UWC issued 'passes' to workers in essential services, but elsewhere restricted freedom of movement through barricades in the areas it controlled. It also restricted the opening of shops in those areas. Two key elements ensured the success of the strike above all others. The first was the support of the power workers as electricity cuts quickly brought Northern Ireland to a standstill. The second was the presence of loyalist paramilitaries, who in the first days of the strike manned the road-blocks and, thereby, deployed an appropriate level of intimidation that ensured middle-class acquiescence. Although the strike quickly gained the almost total support of the Unionist community after the first few days, initially its success was by no means certain – Paisley, for one, had absented himself on pastoral duty in Canada.

In addition to the general climate of intimidation, thirty-four people were killed in no-warning car bombs in Dublin and Monaghan on 17 May, which immediately aroused suspicions of British collusion with loyalist paramilitaries in setting off the bombs. The remaining stories of the strike can be quickly told. First, while the army feared a 'two-front war', they also did not possess the know-how or the requisite numbers of engineers to get the power stations up and running again. Second, Harold Wilson's condemnation of the strikers as 'spongers' in a special television broadcast not only fortified their resolve, but also reflected the ambiguous relationship between the new Labour administration and the (Conservative-designed) power-sharing executive. Finally, threatened with the total failure of emergency service provision, Faulkner resigned on 28 May.

The emergence of the UWC and the success of the strike created an impression that the executive would have succeeded had it not been for the strike. Both nationalists and unionists blamed the recently elected Labour government. John Hume, for example, argued that they:

> backed down to the strike instead of standing firm as they should have done … Unfortunately, this political cowardice of the government was a disaster because extreme unionism or loyalism was encouraged in its belief that it could henceforth resist and jettison any British policy for Northern Ireland which involved conceding power to the minority.[31]

Hume not only blamed the government for failing to stand firm; the conclusions he drew were to influence profoundly the future direction of SDLP policy towards Northern Ireland. Instead of looking for dialogue with unionism, the SDLP would begin to concentrate on exerting pressure on the British government – via allies in Washington and Dublin – to impose a solution. Hume summarised the conclusions that were drawn: 'They [the unionists] have to be brought to realise that they cannot have matters all their own way.'[32] Faulkner, for example, complained that the new government did not nurture the Conservative-designed institutions in a careful manner. On the other hand, Unionists took from the strike the vindication that, while power sharing was desirable in principle, it made no sense to share power with those who wanted to end the Union.

Along with the tendency to blame the Labour administration, many commentators and political protagonists have claimed that the power-sharing experiment failed because the Council of Ireland was too strong. This explanation stresses that Dublin had listened too much to John Hume and should have 'settled' for power sharing.[33] This view has been shared not only by unionist and nationalist participants in the executive such as McIvor, Fitt, and Devlin, but also continues to inform some contemporary political analysis: thus, if Dublin 'had not taken its cue from Hume, it would have done well to accept an advisory council, granting [Dublin] an initially limited role in Northern Ireland's affairs'.[34] Hindsight is not always twenty-twenty though, especially when political commentators refuse to examine the available historical sources. The archives reveal three main findings:

1 Neither Dublin nor the SDLP had any intention of 'settling' for power sharing.
2 Faulkner had supported cross-border bodies since at least September 1971 and agreed to executive functions before the Sunningdale conference in October 1973.
3 Unionist unease with *sharing power* with the SDLP, regardless of the Irish dimension, was widespread and deeply embedded.

Therefore, given the extent of divisions within Northern Ireland society, it was unlikely that power sharing could have succeeded at this time. The tendency to concentrate on the events of 1974 and, in particular, the ill-defined Council of Ireland is, however, understandable: we often draw conclusions from the most evident facts and ignore underlying trends. The principal lesson that we can draw from Sunningdale is not that a different decision – a reduced Irish dimension or having power sharing without the Council of Ireland – would have produced a different outcome. Sunningdale was not a missed opportunity precisely because the gulf between the two communities was too great to begin with.

The tendency to see Sunningdale as something that would have 'worked' had alternative choices been made is forgivable in the accounts of the main protagonists, since people who experience events at first hand are affected in different ways and draw different conclusions from those more removed from the scene. What is less forgivable is the perpetuation of these conclusions by contemporary commentators simply because a longer-term perspective – that is, one that takes into account the events of the years leading up to 1974 – reveals that Sunningdale was unlikely to succeed. This perspective is supported by the historical evidence – unionists had an embedded distrust of power sharing while nationalists held a deep-seated desire for gradual reunification. The problem for the government was that that gulf had widened due to the events of May 1974. Thus, while the SDLP, Brian Faulkner, and the UUUC drew different conclusions from the strike, for its part, Westminster was left with the same dilemma it faced in March 1972 – how to intervene without making the situation any worse.

3

'Refereeing the fight': the limitations of British intervention, 1974–85

The limitations of British intervention

The conceit that Britain had done all it could do and that the Northern Ireland conflict was essentially about ethnic and religious bigotry permeated the Westminster policymaking machine in the aftermath of the Ulster Workers' Council strike. Reflecting on the aftermath of the May strike, the Secretary of State Merlyn Rees detected an emerging sense of what he called 'Ulster nationalism'. He believed that this new sense of identity should be nurtured: since 'the British cannot solve the Irish problem … it would be better to let them have a shot at it themselves'.[1] As Harold Wilson's press secretary, Joe Haines, later remarked: 'From then on, we were not even refereeing the fight, only holding the coats while the religious factions get on with it.'[2] As a result of such thinking, two dominant themes emerged in the British approach to Northern Ireland during the second half of the 1970s – increased spending in social security and fair employment legislation, and a reduction of Britain's political involvement. This had the knock-on effect of increasing Northern Ireland's financial dependence on the UK (in other words, the 'British subvention'). However, any benefits accruing from the attempted economic modernisation of Northern Ireland were undermined by the political uncertainty that continued to reign over the perception of British ambiguity. As two prominent historians of the conflict pointed out, the net result of British policymaking during the latter 1970s was to 'manipulate and domesticate rather than transform or eradicate' the underlying societal divisions.[3]

The ambiguities inherent in British policymaking arose from the fact that the complexity of the Northern Ireland conflict created a multitude of 'solutions'. On 30 May 1974, for example, Harold Wilson asked his senior ministers to consider what he referred to as the 'nuclear option' of withdrawal – something he was to return to at the beginning of 1976.[4] The Northern Ireland Office (NIO), meanwhile, continued to push for a downsizing of Britain's political involvement in the North and from 1975 onwards began to develop various forms of policy initiatives through which 'distancing' could be achieved. This accompanied the growing awareness that devolved power sharing, though desirable in principle, could not be imposed on the North, meaning that British involvement would have to take a different form:

> If we are faced with long-term direct rule, there is much to be said for making it clear that we are embarking on a semi-permanent arrangement rather than a purely temporary one.[5]

One of the principal ways in which the British presence could be reduced, according to the NIO, was through the re-introduction of a majoritarian system. This idea of Unionist rule – albeit tempered by political and economic safeguards for Nationalists – was described by Wilson's senior policy advisor, Bernard Donoughue, as 'totally inadequate' and it was a 'bloody certainty' that it would drive Catholics into the IRA.[6] Donoughue favoured a semi-autonomous Northern Ireland, which would be closer to the South and further from Britain, and which would have 'dominion status' on a par with Canada.[7]

In short, while Westminster maintained a public commitment to restoring devolution, power sharing as such was not a priority. Furthermore, competing viewpoints within government surfaced in several areas including the private discussions with political parties and the Irish government; in the attitude to the proceedings of the inter-party talks which formed the Constitutional Convention (1975–6); and in the decision to hold 'secret' talks with the IRA during its intermittent ceasefire, which began in the final days of 1974 and lasted until late summer 1975 (with the talks continuing into 1976). What this meant was that while Britain could be seen as a 'neutral arbitrator',[8] the arbitration occurred in very much a 'hands-off' style. Indeed, it is probably more accurate – and more helpful – to suggest that British policymaking during the latter 1970s and for much of the early 1980s had no discernible objective, no overarching vision, and very little coherent logic. The only consistent theme was of deleterious ambiguity.

It would be wrong to suggest, however, that British officials and politicians were operating from faulty premises or an underdeveloped understanding of the Northern Ireland conflict. Rather, the ambiguity at the heart of British policymaking was as much a product of the previous attempts to impose power sharing on an unwilling population as much as it was a reflection of the wide divisions within Northern Irish politics. In other words, even if Britain had deployed a long-term and decisive course of action, there was no guarantee that it would have made the situation any better. Thus, it was not merely the case of failing to learn from past 'mistakes'. There was no natural progression from mistakes to solutions, because in essence the problem was not that no single 'solution' existed, but that there were both too many, and none that would not make the situation worse.

The Constitutional Convention, 1975–6

The Constitutional Convention was effectively set up to 'let the Irish sort it out for themselves'. The thinking behind the initiative was to provide a forum in which Northern Ireland's politicians could meet to discuss possible ways out of the political stalemate and to reach agreement on how power could be devolved back to Northern Ireland. The avowed purpose behind the Convention was, therefore, to provide a floor upon which the North's future could be debated and hopefully allow the local politicians to reach some form of agreement around which power could be successfully devolved. A more cynical interpretation – and one that was shared by British policymakers in private discussions – was that the Convention would allow the government to say it was doing all it could to further political accommodation while, at the same time, insulating mainstream British politics from the Northern Ireland question. Since the issues, beliefs, and positions of the local parties had been thrashed out many times in the past and everyone knew each other's basic points of view, few people either within Northern Ireland or in London held out much hope for a successful outcome of the Convention.

The government, however, set out three conditions for any future settlement. First, it had to include 'some form of power sharing and partnership, because no political system will survive, or be supported, unless there is a widespread acceptance of it within the community'. Second, the settlement had to be acceptable to the UK government. Third, the government stated that since Northern Ireland, unlike other parts of the UK, shared a land border and a 'special relationship' with the Republic of Ireland, any settlement had to recognise those facts, thus: 'There is an Irish dimension.'[9] The idea in fact allowed the government to sideline the Northern Irish problem without suffering international condemnation. In what was effectively a win–win situation for Westminster, in the unlikely event that agreement would be reached, devolution could be restored; on the other hand, there was every chance that the local parties would demonstrate to the world high levels of division, intransigence, and primordial contention.

The SDLP was initially reluctant to take part in the experiment following the government's downgrading of executive power sharing to the more ambiguous 'some form'. During the Convention, the party continued to push for a strong Northern Ireland assembly; for 'all sections of the community [to be] represented at government level'; and for cross-border institutions. The party rejected proposals to restore majority rule and questioned whether the UUUC was really against sharing power with republicans or simply with the SDLP. The political points-scoring was in fact a futile exercise because the SDLP had fundamentally underestimated the extent of the government's policy reprioritisation. Unlike the SDLP, the government recognised that the UWC strike had shown that the Unionist population could not be coerced into a political settlement. In this new environment, little could be offered to the SDLP:

> The question is therefore no longer what can be done to satisfy the minority, but what the minority ... are prepared to do to strengthen the hand of HMG in consolidating the political gains won for the minority since 1968.[10]

As the Convention was to demonstrate, neither the SDLP nor the UUUC had engaged in any kind of fundamental rethink following the collapse of the Sunningdale executive. Instead, the earlier policies of each group persisted and became ever more radical. Rather than promoting political dialogue or fostering a potential settlement, the Convention witnessed the further widening of the political gulf in Northern Ireland. Thus while the SDLP continued to insist on executive power sharing to be allocated as a right – that is, by proportional representation – the UUUC continued to push for a majoritarian settlement in which unionists would hold veto powers. In this regard, the UUUC's preferred option was Brian Faulkner's June 1971 ideas – a majoritarian Stormont, based on Westminster practices, with committee seats to be allocated to the 'Opposition' (the SDLP).

In part the continued division was due to the kinds of lessons both the SDLP and the UUUC learned – that the Unionists must be 'faced down' and that majority rule was essential to resist an 'imposed settlement', respectively. These lessons meant that the earlier policies of the UUUC's resistance to power sharing and the SDLP's prioritisation of an Irish dimension were not questioned; rather, they were reinforced by the continued uncertainty over future prospects. This political uncertainty continued to increase due to Westminster's apparent willingness to countenance IRA demands for withdrawal and its demonstrable reluctance to confront the paramilitaries through more hard-line security measures when the killing rate began to spiral once again in the second half of 1975.

Elections to the Convention were held on 1 May 1975. The UUUC completed the demolition of Brian Faulkner's political career, winning forty-seven of the seventy-eight seats to Faulkner's Unionist Party of Northern Ireland's five. The SDLP won seventeen seats; while the Alliance and the NILP won eight and one respectively. The Convention has come to symbolise the poverty and discord that represented Northern Irish

IAN PAISLEY

In a similar manner to John Hume's fashioning of a political persona after the nationalist leader Charles Stewart Parnell, Ian Paisley consciously sought to imitate the early-twentieth-century unionist leader Edward Carson. In particular, Paisley aligned himself with Carson's distrust of the British establishment and his willingness to go to the limits of the law in order to defend the Union. However, for much of his political career this radicalism alienated more unionists than it attracted, and conservative middle-class Protestants together with socialistic working-class loyalists were often repelled by his violent rhetoric and anti-Catholic fundamentalism.

Paisley's contribution to Northern Irish political developments is, therefore, intensely paradoxical: on the one hand, conservative unionists stayed with the moderate Unionist Party because they feared that Britain would abandon the North in the event of a Paisleyite take-over. On the other hand, the Unionist Party's moderation was restrained precisely because of the threat being denounced by Paisley of 'selling-out'.

Paisley founded both the Free Presbyterian Church and the Democratic Unionist Party in his own radical, fundamental image. However, from at least 1998 the DUP took an increasingly pragmatic stance regarding political events, allowing it to become the largest unionist party and allowing Paisley to govern Northern Ireland along with Sinn Féin's Martin McGuinness from May 2007. His resignation in May 2008, amidst reports of general unrest among the ruling elders of the Free Presbyterian Church, indicated that his legacy may be as difficult to define as his career was when he was active.

politics in the period after Sunningdale. In fact agreement was apparently almost reached in private discussions; during which William Craig – a member of the UUUC delegation – broached the idea that a devolved executive could be established following the precedent of the World War II cabinet at Westminster. This would see the restoration of a majoritarian executive (that is, controlled by unionists) but with the SDLP invited to participate for as long as the 'emergency' lasted. This idea of a 'voluntary coalition' was developed by a young academic lawyer and advisor to Craig, David Trimble, but it was rejected by the UUUC following a last-minute intervention from Ian Paisley.

The rationale behind Paisley's intervention was, according to received wisdom, an attempt by the DUP leader to claim a monopolistic control over unionist politics. Thus, Paisley 'saw the opportunity of capitalising on the fear and distrust that was growing up among Unionist supporters for the secret negotiations that appeared to be going on'.[11] In this view, Paisley's decision to oppose a crucial UUUC motion on whether to back the proposal at the beginning of September 1975 was an example of political expediency in that he sought to demolish Craig and relegate the UUP to a subordinate position behind the DUP.

Regardless of the fact that Paisley would not have known the outcome of the open vote – since the UUUC was not a political party but a loose association – in which Craig was comprehensively defeated 37–1, the immediate concern for Ulster Unionists during much of 1975 was not the reaching of political agreement, but rather the British government's relationship with the IRA. In particular, following the IRA's return to violence from August onwards, the priority for unionists was security. For some unionists, the debate over political initiatives merely served to distract attention from the key problem of restoring a degree of normality to day-to-day living in Northern Ireland. Thus, during the debate on the voluntary coalition proposal, Enoch Powell, a high-profile Conservative-defector to the Ulster Unionist benches at Westminster claimed that:

the Convention now is contributing to the bloodshed. It is of the highest interest that the proceedings of the Convention should be brought to a conclusion as speedily as possible, whatever the result should be.[12]

The escalation of the IRA's campaign during the summer of 1975 contributed to a hardening of the UUUC's attitude towards political compromise. Among other numerous incidents, that escalation witnessed the shooting of a four-year-old girl, Siobhan McCabe, by a stray bullet, when an anti-internment rally descended into rioting in West Belfast on 10 August. On 13 August, the IRA killed five Protestants in a bomb attack on the Mountainview Tavern bar on the Shankill Road, while on 1 September the IRA shot dead four men in an attack on an Orange Hall in Newtownhamilton.

The driving force behind the IRA's escalation was the so-called 'Balcombe Street gang', who were responsible for at least sixteen killings in England during 1974 and 1975. Their tactics often included no-warning bombings on pubs and they were implicated in the bombings for which innocent men and women (including the high-profile cases of the colloquially named 'Guildford Four' and the 'Birmingham Six') were wrongly convicted. In addition to the rise in republican violence, loyalists also stepped up their campaign. In one notorious incident, a UVF gang, some of whom were also part-time members of the Ulster Defence Regiment (UDR), staged a bogus UDR roadblock near Newry on 31 July with the intention of loading a bomb on to the Miami Showband's van to make it seem as if the band were transporting explosives. When the bomb prematurely exploded, killing two UVF men, the paramilitaries decided to kill the surviving witnesses. The gang shot three members of the band and seriously injured a fourth; the fifth member was blown through a hedge by the blast and managed to hide during the ferocious gunfire.

Paramilitary violence continued and, between 1 August and 1 September, republicans killed twenty people while loyalists killed seventeen.

As with Sunningdale, Craig's voluntary coalition idea was unlikely to have succeeded in the historical climate of the time. Certainly, there is little evidence that the SDLP would have agreed to the idea. While the SDLP delegation *was* amenable to radical initiatives – in particular, the idea that a 'US-style' presidential system could be established – the party's supporters were not. It is far from certain that Craig's idea would have fulfilled these conditions, entailing as it did a subordinate role for the SDLP within any devolved executive. Having already enjoyed executive responsibilities as of right in 1974, it is difficult to see how or why the SDLP would have settled for a less favourable offer the following year.

The UUUC refused to go as far as giving the SDLP an executive voice in the running of Northern Ireland and rejected Craig's idea that nationalists could sit in a unionist-dominated cabinet until the security situation had improved. The UUUC in fact, was only prepared to go as far as offering the SDLP seats at the committee, rather than the cabinet level, which, in effect, represented a reprise of Brian Faulkner's offer to the SDLP in June 1971 (see chapter 2). Why this plan should have appeared as being capable of restoring Stormont in 1975–6 when it was not enough to save Stormont in 1972 is not immediately apparent. The persistence of the UUUC's committee seats policy however, does demonstrate two characteristics of the UUUC: first, that it had little if anything to provide beyond resisting what it perceived to be an attempt to impose power sharing in 1974; second, that security concerns rather than political initiatives remained central to unionist thinking during the post-Stormont era.

The Convention was wound down definitively in March 1976 having failed to reach any kind of cross-community consensus. What can be said with certainty is that Craig's repudiation by the UUUC ended his political career. His Vanguard Party fractured, and, like Faulkner before him, his initiative demonstrated the difficulties involved in getting too far ahead of grass-roots support. As Paisley pointed out to one official: 'Craig's proposal should never have been pushed since it had no hope of success. The political history of Ulster was littered with the discarded leaders of unionism who had tried to do the same.'[13]

Northern Ireland's politicians continued to pursue much the same policies in the second half of the 1970s as they did in the first half. John Hume replaced Gerry Fitt as leader of the SDLP in 1979 and continued to press for a strong role for Dublin in the affairs of Northern Ireland. In particular, Hume used the example of the European Community as a model of power sharing and cooperation, and looked to key contacts in the United States – including Edward Kennedy and the Speaker of the House of Representatives, Tip O'Neill – to exert pressure on the White House for reform and investment.

Despite his calls for dialogue and reconciliation, Hume made little headway in convincing unionists that what he called a 'new Ireland, an agreed Ireland' would be any different from the old project of dissolving the Union by stealth. Thus his insight that proper institutional arrangements could accommodate divisive viewpoints – as in the European Community – actually served to undercut unionist suspicions by portraying them as unreasonable. Having failed to persuade unionists of his vision, he claimed that unless Britain became a 'persuader' for Irish unity, unionists would never agree to negotiate as equals. The problem for unionists was that Hume's idea that an equal starting point required giving up the constitutional link with Britain – this meant that they would have effectively conceded to the principle of reunification before dialogue began.

In a similar fashion, Ulster unionism pursued internal debates that held little interest for the Irish nationalists. The Unionist Party threatened to split apart over the question of whether Northern Ireland would be better off pursuing some form of devolution or entering into a more fully integrated relationship with Britain. James Molyneaux, who assumed the party leadership in 1979, favoured a continuation of direct rule, with enhanced local administration, and strengthened links to British politics, primarily through the allocation of more Westminster seats. The UUUC, meanwhile, had itself split apart in 1977 following a disastrous re-run of the UWC strike by Paisley in May – which was condemned by the Unionist Party and the Orange Order and failed to attract the support of the power workers – and the revelations that the Unionist Party had been engaging in secret talks with the SDLP during the summer months.

The government's reaction to these talks was decidedly tepid: the then head of the Northern Ireland Office, Brian Cubbon, warned that the Unionist Party could use the talks to raise its profile within Ulster unionism, and provoke the DUP into mobilising in opposition. In Cubbon's terms, the talks could concoct a 'flimsy scheme' whose object would be 'a way of dumping on our lap the problem of coping with Paisley'.[14]

Whitehall and the IRA

Even before the establishment of the Constitutional Convention, the British government had begun a serious reappraisal of what direct rule should mean in practice. By the late spring of 1975, for example, NIO briefings stressed the inability of the government to 'impose a solution',[15] and officials advised embarking on a policy of what they called 'distancing'. The alternative – enhanced integration into the UK system –

was ruled out almost right from the start of this reappraisal. Instead, government officials favoured placing policy implementation on 'a more local footing':

> By 'distancing' is meant the reduction of our commitments in Northern Ireland in constitutional, military, and economic terms – and the relegation of the Northern Ireland problem to a place of lesser importance than it currently occupies on the British political scene.[16]

The NIO did not rule out the possibility of 'majority rule' with 'minority safeguards'; however, power sharing on the 1974 model was not a priority. Rather, the main concern was to reduce British exposure in Northern Ireland and minimise the risk of international embarrassment. However, Britain's 'hands-off' approach meant a diminution of the importance of both the Irish dimension and executive power sharing – a development that perturbed the SDLP and led Dublin to avoid any actions that might increase Britain's desire to leave. Indeed, when the Irish Minister for Foreign Affairs, Garret FitzGerald, complained to the Northern Ireland Secretary of State, Merlyn Rees, that the republican leader Dáithí Ó Conaill had been arrested in Dublin while carrying a document purporting to be the terms of a truce, the Secretary of State's denial of secret negotiations appeared neither diplomatic nor politic but merely dishonest and gauche. So worried was the Irish government that Britain would withdraw from Northern Ireland, or, in its words, shuffle 'off the Northern coil', that the Department of Foreign Affairs began to prepare contingency notes on withdrawal scenarios.[17]

The reason why Britain was so anxious to talk to the IRA was because it discerned the possibility for political progress, in the light of the IRA's decision to call a ceasefire. For their part, the IRA had called the ceasefire for several reasons. First, republicans believed that the 'inaction and vagueness of British government policy' was a deliberate ploy on the part of the British to increase unionist obduracy and facilitate the conditions for withdrawal.[18] Second, for republicans, the UWC strike demonstrated a new potential within working-class loyalism to break with the unionist elites and attack the British government. In addition, the fact that republican and loyalist communities shared similar concerns over internment and an increased army presence in their locales increased the sense of rapprochement. Furthermore, republicans had been in secret contact with senior NIO officials and Michael Oatley of the British Secret Intelligence Service since the ceasefire of 1972.[19] Following a series of meetings with church leaders in late 1974, the IRA extended its holiday ceasefire to the end of January 1975, before announcing an indefinite ceasefire on 9 February. Of much greater importance was the apparent willingness of the British government to politicise the republican and loyalist paramilitary groupings. Sinn Féin and the UVF were briefly de-proscribed in a move which Rees hoped would lead to a speedy end of the conflict and perhaps a convergence of working-class interests. The latter envisaged outcome was wishful thinking on the British part, as Protestants and Catholics remained deeply entrenched in their ethnic, national, and religious camps, with little serious prospect of a revitalised class consciousness. The socialist basis of the Northern Ireland Labour movement – formerly invested in the NILP – had by now been absorbed into other parties such as the DUP, SDLP, and Alliance Party.

   The republican movement was mistaken in its assessment of the long-term objectives of British policymaking simply because there was none to speak of. Republicans mistakenly equated the hesitancy and ambiguity in the day-to-day delivery of policy with a certain desire to withdraw. Indeed, London encouraged this interpretation in the hope that, by stringing the movement along, it would eventually demoralise and defeat it. As an indication of good faith, the government went some way towards meeting a twelve-point programme drawn up by the IRA. Among the measures the government agreed to were the setting up of 'incident centres', which would be staffed by Sinn Féin; the withdrawal of the army to barracks; and the granting of immunity from arrest of specific individuals.

Although the IRA ceasefire had effectively ended by the summer of 1975, Rees allowed talks to continue until well into 1976.[20] During this period, Wilson became increasingly apprehensive about the direction of events in the North. He had dallied with the idea of withdrawal following the UWC strike in 1974, and he returned to the idea in January 1976 in a memorandum entitled 'Apocalyptic note'.[21] In this top-secret memorandum, the prime minister alerted his immediate advisors to the possibility of large-scale industrial unrest or the escalation of terrorist violence – either of which, he said, would completely undermine Britain's ability to exercise control of law and order in the region. The 'only solution', he said, was 'withdrawal and the abnegation of responsibilities for the interior affairs of Northern Ireland in the wider international community. It would mean clear, legal, constitutional separation.' Wilson claimed that the 'purblind fanaticism' of sections of the population had brought matters to a head and created a situation in which a 'crunch' was imminent.

Alarmed at the prime minister's train of thought and worried that he might take precipitate action by bringing his concerns before the wider cabinet, his cabinet secretary (and head of the civil service), John Hunt, hastily intervened by suggesting that both he and the head of the Northern Ireland civil service, Frank Cooper, could come 'to have a word'.[22] Although the matter ended with Hunt's intervention, the memorandum is revealing in at least two respects. First, it indicates something of Wilson's preoccupations during his final months in office. Second, it demonstrates once again the brittle and ad hoc nature of Whitehall's approach to Northern Ireland during the 1970s – and that, while all options were 'on the table', the very fact of there being so many cluttered and disparate alternatives meant that they cancelled each other out, thus maintaining an overriding and self-reproducing sense of ambiguity and uncertainty.

After the events of 1974–6 (namely, the collapse of the power-sharing executive, the collapse of the Convention, and the collapse of the IRA ceasefire), Westminster shied away from imposing any major policy initiatives. Instead, policymakers sought to implement direct rule on an ad hoc basis according to the principles laid down in a June 1977 directive:

> The defeat of terrorism, agreement on durable and acceptable constitutional arrangements, and the improvement of the economy are interdependent, and lie at the heart of the government's policy.[23]

The new Secretary of State, Roy Mason, personified this new minimalist approach. Mason, who replaced Rees in September 1976, was a high-profile member of the Labour government: a former Home Affairs Minister, as Secretary of State for Defence he was also responsible for authorising the deployment of the SAS into Northern Ireland earlier that year. Mason had grown up in the coal-mining region of South Yorkshire and was himself a former miner. Whereas Rees had often vacillated, Mason adopted a decisive and hard-line approach. Thus he told the Labour Party conference in the autumn of 1976 that: 'Ulster has had enough of initiatives, White Papers and legislation for the time being, and now needed to be governed firmly and fairly'.[24]

Mason had already stunned local reporters at his first press conference as Secretary of State when he claimed that 'Unemployment, little new investment, too many businesses closing down, these are the questions that must receive priority'.[25] The dire state of the Northern Ireland economy almost justified Mason's hyperbolic attempt to ignore the problems of political stalemate, inter-communal division, and terrorist violence. The long-term decline of Northern Ireland's staple industries – shipbuilding, agriculture, and textiles – had been temporarily offset by the establishment of multinational factories in the 1960s. However, with the worldwide recession of the 1970s, the escalation of sectarian strife, and the North's peripheral location, these businesses began to close down. As international investment declined, unemployment rose and the Northern Ireland average remained the worst in the UK at around fourteen per cent from the late 1970s onwards. Economics directly affected the political situation by contributing decisively to Catholic alienation. Thus, in the 1970s Catholics were more likely to be less well-off than Protestants and more likely to be employed in industries with lower wages and more unemployment (such as construction) than Protestants, who were more likely to be found in industries such as engineering. Again, while Catholics were 2.6 times as likely to be unemployed as Protestants in 1971, by 1981, this figure had marginally improved to 2.4 times.[26]

Mason continued to implement Rees's ideas on having the local Northern Irish forces – the RUC and the UDR – as the main agents in the fight against the IRA. 'Ulsterisation', as this policy became known, not only served to reduce the exposure of 'British' troops on the streets, it also contributed significantly to a further deterioration of community relations in Northern Ireland. Since the local security forces were overwhelmingly staffed by Protestants, Ulsterisation simply raised the ethnic stakes – Protestants in the RUC were policing Catholics and Catholics in the IRA were killing the police. Allegations of RUC brutality towards prisoners, coupled with Mason's hardline approach (as he explained in his memoirs, 'I had been harassing the IRA with as much vigour as was legally acceptable in a liberal democracy') simply added to the mix. The upshot was that, on the one hand moderate nationalists grew even more disenchanted with what they perceived to be the 'structural bias' of direct rule.[27] On the other hand, the IRA reorganised its operational structure along cellular lines and under a new Northern-based leadership. These 'cells' operated in different areas across the North on a largely autonomous basis, thereby creating a more responsive and improvisatory response to events. The other advantage was that volunteers would know only other members of their cell with each cell's leader knowing people further up the chain of command. Although this was a deliberate attempt to try to thwart British infiltration of the organisation, as the ever-growing list of double agents who come to light in various leaks demonstrates, British intelligence services had penetrated all levels of the IRA by the 1980s.

The series of revelations in recent years concerning the nature and extent of the police's network of IRA informers suggests that the restructuring process did little to insulate the republican movement. While the effect of British infiltration of the IRA can only be surmised at present, a historical consensus is beginning to form around the second strand of the republican rethink – namely, the emergence of a more politically conscious strategy. Whereas previously Sinn Féin – the 'political wing' of the movement – had been subservient to the IRA – the 'military wing' – this relationship began to change, slowly and almost imperceptibly from 1977. The first indication was a speech given by the veteran republican, Jimmy Drumm – but drafted by Gerry Adams and his public relations specialist, Danny Morrison – at the annual republican commemoration at Bodenstown churchyard. At first glance, the speech seemed to criticise the fundamentals of republican beliefs: thus, Drumm criticised the view that 'liberation' could come about through force of arms alone. However, this was not a call to end the violence, rather 'Drumm's' alternative was merely to begin to raise economic issues in tandem with the armed campaign.

In short, republicans had reached an impasse and were looking to find anything upon which they could base their 'struggle' other than the legacy of their own perceived sacrifices. Thus as one senior leader remarked in 1978 when asked whether the campaign had been worth it: 'Of course not. Virtually nothing has been achieved. We can't give up now and admit that men and women who were sent to their graves died for nothing.'[28] The fact that the rethink was strategic rather than a fundamental overhaul was demonstrated in the continued violence. For example, there had already been over a hundred bombs planted that year before the firebombing of the La Mon Hotel in east Belfast in February 1978, where twelve Protestants were burned to death in the IRA attack so horrendously that their remains could only be identified forensically.

The hunger strikes to the Anglo-Irish Agreement

As part of the British government's own restructuring of security arrangements, in 1976 it ended internment and began to phase out the 'special category' status for paramilitary prisoners, which had been introduced by Whitelaw in 1972. Republicans resisted this attempt to 'criminalise' what they perceived to be a just war and from the autumn of 1976 prisoners refused to wear prison clothes. In response the authorities confined the prisoners to their cells and cancelled remission – effectively doubling the time spent in gaol. Republican prisoners began what became known as the 'blanket protest' by refusing to wear the prison clothing and refusing to carry out the prescribed prison activities. This protest was supported by a concerted effort by the IRA outside the gaols to target prison officers, resulting in nineteen being killed. However, having made little headway, the prisoners decided to raise the stakes by refusing to leave their cells. Thus, the blanket protest mutated into a 'no wash' protest. When prison officers refused to empty the chamber pots, the revolt turned into what became known as the 'dirty protest' – with the remains of the uncollected food and excrement being spread on the cell walls. The tit-for-tat continued to escalate and the prison authorities responded with forced baths and haircuts – complaints of beatings and brutality followed accordingly.

Despite a growing international condemnation of the way in which the British were handling the protest, the prisoners elicited little support from the Northern nationalist community, apart from the traditional working–class republican strongholds of west Belfast, south Armagh, and Derry. The final tactic that remained to the prisoners in the stand–off was the hunger strike. Yet when seven prisoners embarked on a hunger strike in October 1980, not only did they fail to elicit widespread support, the British also remained implacable. The new prime minister, Margaret Thatcher, had recently lost her close friend and Northern Ireland advisor, Airey Neave, to a car bomb; in addition, a cousin of the Queen, Earl Mountbatten, was killed in the Republic on the same day (27 August 1979) as the bombing of eighteen soldiers outside Warrenpoint, County Down. With one of the hunger strikers close to death, republicans called off the protest in December 1980. When it became evident that the British had not conceded their demands, the prisoners commenced a second hunger strike on 1 March 1981. The tactic this time was for unmarried prisoners to begin a hunger strike at intervals thus lengthening the protest and amplifying its impact with a steady stream of deaths – the IRA killed forty-five people in 1980 and sixty-nine people in 1981.

In March 1981, the Northern Ireland Westminster seat of Fermanagh-South Tyrone became vacant and was won by the first hunger striker, Bobby Sands. Although he stood unaffiliated to Sinn Féin, his success demonstrated new political possibilities to the movement. As the strike continued two further prisoners were returned to the Irish Parliament and Sands' agent held on to the Westminster seat following his death. Indeed, the leadership of the movement outside the gaol was quick to recognise the new openings created and cynically sought to capitalise on the hunger strikers' sacrifices. Thus, as one of the senior inmates involved in the strike has recently revealed, after the fourth death the British made an improved offer that 'was sufficient for us to settle the dispute honourably'. This included the restoration of remission, the granting of the right to wear their own clothes, and concessions on work and visits – all the prisoners' demands apart from the right to free association.

On the outside, however, Sinn Féin leader Gerry Adams vacillated and the Army Council – the IRA's governing body – vetoed the deal.[29] Despite an almost total loss of prisoners' morale and the imminent death of the hunger striker Joe McDonnell (who was within days of dying when the offer was made), the leadership apparently calculated that the publicity of allowing the strike to continue should take priority. McDonnell and five other hunger strikers died (bringing the total to ten) before the prisoners' families were able to intervene to bring an end to the protest. The concessions available after the fourth death were quietly implemented in the aftermath of the strike.

The two governments were alarmed at the turn of events. In 1982 Thatcher's Secretary of State for Northern Ireland, James Prior, had convened another Assembly to discuss constitutional options, and while nationalists decided to boycott it over the fact that the Irish dimension was not up for negotiation, both the SDLP and Sinn Féin contested the election. In what was effectively Sinn Féin's first election contest since the 1950s, it won 10.1% of the vote compared with 18.8% for the SDLP. In short, one in every three Catholics voted for the militants. On the unionist side, the Ulster Unionist Party won 29.7% while the DUP won twenty-three per cent of the vote – a result that was seen in some quarters as evidence of unionism turning towards a moderate position after the period of uncertainty inspired by the hunger strikes.

This was the context in which Britain and Ireland began the search for an alternative political strategy, and which culminated in the Anglo-Irish Agreement of November 1985 (see below for further details of the Agreement). The British were encouraged to pursue closer cooperation following the return of Garret FitzGerald – perceived as a political moderate – as the Irish Premier, in December 1982. Although FitzGerald had earlier made overtures towards Ulster unionism, his main Northern priority upon his election was to tackle the alienation of moderate nationalists and to stop the growth of Sinn Féin.[30] Following discussions with John Hume, FitzGerald convened the New Ireland Forum to debate the future of relations on the island in 1983. Although unionists briefly visited the Forum, its proceedings and conclusions were markedly nationalistic in tenor – stressing the desirability of a single unified state.

Despite this, the experiment can be seen as signifying an increased openness at least to consider the idea that Unionists felt themselves to be British and that a stable Northern Ireland depended on that recognition.[31] John Hume's American allies also influenced a more direct intergovernmental approach – the Reagan administration offered Tip O'Neill a stronger Irish policy if he dropped his objections to funding the Nicaraguan contras.[32] An additional factor was Thatcher's concern that the Republic was not doing enough to tackle IRA terrorism.[33] Although tentative negotiations had been taking place with the

South since 1983, Thatcher became increasingly convinced of the need for enhanced security arrangements following the IRA bombing of the Grand Hotel in Brighton during the annual Conservative Party conference in October 1984, in which she herself narrowly escaped death. Thatcher's strategy was to link these security concerns to the offer of a greater political role for the South, together with the possibility of a devolved power-sharing settlement in the North. What these various strands reveal is that the Anglo-Irish Agreement was not the product of an overarching vision for Northern Ireland. Rather it was the untidy product of both governments having to operate within what one political scientist has called 'the parameters of the possible'.[34]

The Anglo-Irish Agreement (AIA) was signed by the two governments in November 1985. Although the Irish government consulted John Hume during the negotiations leading up to the signing, Ulster unionists were effectively sidelined and kept in the dark. The main features of the Anglo-Irish Agreement were set out in its fourth article – security coopera-tion; a consultative (though not executive) role for Dublin in the shape of the Intergovernmental Conference; and the possibility of restoring power-sharing devolution. In addition, the Agreement provided for Dublin officials to have a perma-nent presence in Northern Ireland in the form of the 'Maryfield secretariat'. While that presence was far from the joint authority role envisaged by the New Ireland Forum, it did afford Dublin a say, for the first time, in how the North was being run. As Paul Bew has recently pointed out, the Agreement changed the face of Northern Irish politics by ushering in 'an era of direct rule with a green tinge'.[35] Even if Margaret Thatcher had been correct in claiming that the Intergovernmental Conference could be 'knocked out' by the establishment of power sharing, the provision of an institutional role for Dublin effectively militated against the possibility that devolution would be restored: having gained Dublin involvement, the SDLP had little incentive to reduce Dublin's role through an internal power-sharing settlement; meanwhile, unionists had little incentive to talk unless Dublin's role was reduced.

4

The peace process: 1985–98

Responses to the Anglo-Irish Agreement

For Northern nationalists the Anglo-Irish Agreement (AIA) had two main effects. First, it encouraged them to build on Dublin's new institutional role by pursuing greater Southern involvement in Northern Ireland. Second, it discouraged them from pursuing any strategies that might endanger that priority – in other words, it provided a barrier against engagement with unionism.[1] However, while the Agreement militated against a power-sharing rapprochement, and provided the basis for nationalist policy convergence, that process of convergence was less than smooth. Long-term policy goals and constitutional bargaining did occur, as Northern nationalists began to approach the prospects of devolved government in the 1990s with a strategy based on encouraging closer institutional, political, and cultural ties with the Republic of Ireland. This was a strategy that was entirely consistent with the historical development of modern Irish nationalism since the early 1970s.

An influential interpretation of the peace process is that, in the 1980s, the British government, under the tutelage of John Hume and Garret FitzGerald, eventually 'learned' how to manage the Northern Ireland conflict by rectifying its past failures.[2] Although this narrative seems to be straightforward and commonsensical, in fact, the idea that Britain gradually learned how to manage Northern Ireland through indefatigable prodding by Irish nationalists is tenable only if we completely disregard the available historical evidence.[3] Certainly, a defining characteristic of Irish nationalism is its constant prodding of successive British governments. However, it is also the case that Britain reluctantly refused to move beyond the 'principle of consent' – namely, the recognition that any change in Northern Ireland's status would have to be endorsed democratically – and take on the mantle nationalists demanded of being a 'persuader' for Irish unity. The 1998 Agreement embodied the principle of consent and, therefore, a strong argument can be made that, rather than Britain moving under pressure from Irish national- ism, it was Irish nationalists who eventually and reluctantly came to accept the constitutional arrangements, albeit for the time being. This dynamic – of nationalists coming further into the Northern state, while at the same time seeking to move beyond it to closer union with the South – characterises the instability at the heart of the peace process.

Indeed, the Anglo-Irish Agreement was instrumental in establishing that dynamic, providing as it did a working frame- work through which nationalists could bring their grievances to the British government and seek constant redress and reform – from issues concerning public appointments to policing and security arrangements. For John Hume, the Anglo-Irish Agreement pointed towards an intergovernmental 'framework' in which nationalists' and unionists' grievances could be addressed. He later claimed that:

> Unionist politicians seemed to object because membership of the UK would no longer be solely on the terms demanded by them. They opposed it because it also gave recognition to the nationalist identity and the reality of the rightful interest of Southern Ireland in the affairs of the North.[4]

However, as with the party's approach to power sharing in 1973, the SDLP prioritised the Irish dimension over any internal settlement in their talks with unionists in Duisburg, West Germany, in October 1988. The talks failed due to the fact that 'Hume's single-mindedness kept him committed to integrating Sinn Féin into an overall political settlement'.[5] Arguably, Hume's courtship of Adams was a strategic and ideological mistake: not only did it give Sinn Féin a degree of credibility they had hitherto lacked, but it also militated against the party's hopes of persuading Protestants to join them in negotiating what Hume himself had termed a 'new Ireland'.

For its part, Ulster Unionism went into something akin to collective shock. Its leaders – Molyneaux and Paisley – had been kept in the dark during the negotiations. One MP, Harold McCusker, told the House of Commons that he 'never knew what desolation felt like until he read the agreement' and claimed that his constituents would be 'Irish-British hybrids'. In direct response to the Agreement, Unionists mobilised several hundred thousand supporters in a mass rally outside Belfast City Hall on 23 November 1985. Ian Paisley whipped the crowd into emotional hysteria and denounced the Agreement with the line: 'we say never, never, never, never', which promptly became the rallying call for Unionist opposition to the Agreement. Moreover, the slogan 'Ulster Says No' drove the campaign forward and served to encapsulate how Unionist critiques of the AIA were 'based around the assumption that the Agreement had altered the terms of the Union, without their consent'.[6] The AIA also provoked a direct constitutional response from Unionist politicians who used the resignation of their respective Westminster parliamentary teams to force by-elections in January 1986. In effect the by-elections served as a mini-referendum on the AIA, but led to only a slight increase in the Unionist vote.[7] Each of the fourteen UUP and DUP candidates stood on an anti-AIA ticket. Indeed the DUP's stock had fallen by almost two per cent among the unionist electorate – with Paisley's rhetoric of a 'Third Force' alienating not only mainstream unionist sensibilities but large swathes of loyalist opinion supportive of the existing paramilitary structures built up around the UDA and UVF.

Unlike at Sunningdale, there were no real visible institutions to attack or any avenues for appeal – the Agreement largely existed as a set of relationships on paper between two sovereign governments. Thus, despite mass rallies and the mass resignation of unionist MPs, the Agreement was largely fireproof. As with the unionists, although for completely different reasons, Irish nationalists also had little incentive to look for restored devolution. John Hume had finally won a role for the Irish government in the North; and while this was much less than what was hoped for in 1973–4, it was still a major step forward in nationalists' eyes and something on which to build. In the short term at least, therefore, the Agreement's contribution to ending the Northern Ireland conflict was negligible and, in many ways – not least in terms of community relations – it could actually be seen to have contributed to the perpetuation of violence.

Despite the near-total alienation of the unionist community, the AIA created several benefits for the British and Irish states. For example, it allowed the British government to alter its strategic relationship with the Republic of Ireland by inviting its input on several matters previously regarded as constitution-ally sacrosanct. The trade-off in all of this was the envisaged improvement in the security situation, which allowed London to seek consensus on its idea for a security band around the border counties. In theory, if not in practice, this made available the possibility of freeing up extradition arrangements between the two states and would have permitted British forces legitimately to cross the border, for example, in pursuit of republican terrorists. The Agreement did help to lay the foundations for a greater cooperation that eventually became a prominent feature of the peace process and the premierships of Prime Minister Tony Blair and Bertie Ahern a decade later.[8]

The Sinn Féin peace strategy

While the Anglo-Irish Agreement provided an incentive for the IRA to give up its armed struggle and pursue more constitutional methods, as the previous chapter pointed out, key elements within the republican leadership recognised the limitations of the armed struggle from the early to mid 1970s. Although there was a political and historical logic behind republicans' decision to abandon the armed campaign, that decision was, however, the result of a cumulative and nuanced process. In other words, the persistence of underlying end goals implies that the move towards politics simply represents a strategic shift in means used to achieve them; thereby suggesting that talk of a 'settlement' may in fact be premature. Rather than settlement or accommodation, it may, therefore, be more accurate to think of the peace process as simply a 'détente' or 'cold war' between deep-seated rivals.

The investigative work of the journalist Ed Moloney subverts the idea that the SDLP leadership, in concert with Southern politicians, created the 'peace process'. Moloney points out that Gerry Adams began drawing up an alternative to the armed campaign as early as 1982; and describes how private talks between Adams and the west Belfast priest, Alex Reid, resulted in the emergence of a growing acceptance within republicanism of the possibility of calling off the armed campaign in favour of a political one. The decision to enter electoral politics in the aftermath of the hunger-strike mobilisation did not simply provide Sinn Féin with a second front. In fact, the 'armalite-and-ballot-box' strategy (a phrase coined by Sinn Féin publicist, Danny

Morrison) also revealed the 'popular disenchantment with the IRA's violence'.[9]

Moloney also alleges that, as early as 1986 Adams, the new Sinn Féin President, sent a secret communiqué to the British Secretary of State Tom King, in which he asked several pointed questions about the British position on Ireland. He alleges that Adams was employing language that was not drastically out of sync with the thinking of hard-line IRA hawks at the time, but that it was also fully consistent with the emphasis republicans were now placing on to the utility of political struggle. Yet Moloney is perhaps a little too overzealous in stressing Adams' Machiavellian credentials – the urban areas in which the Provisionals' hard-core supporters lived had begun to experience the benefits of inward investment in local businesses through a dedicated policy by British ministers.[10] Understandably, the inhabitants of those areas were reluctant to see jobs, shops, and improved quality of life habitually threatened by republican bombs and British Army shootings.

Although Sinn Féin's electoral surge had begun to level off at just over ten per cent by the time the Anglo-Irish Agreement was signed, by representing a 'gain' for constitutional national-ists, the Agreement helped to constrain further growth. John Hume certainly believed that the Agreement had transformed Northern Irish politics, proclaiming that it had 'lanced the Protestant boil' and that unionists would be forced to negotiate by the end of 1986.[11] Unionist disillusionment was not the only reason that that scenario did not pan out the way Hume envisioned. In fact, the anti-power-sharing logic of the Agreement allowed both Hume and Adams to enter into a joint dialogue with the objective of 'identifying a common strategy on bringing about Irish unity, and also on issues affecting nation-alists in Northern Ireland'.[13]

The Hume–Adams talks were prefaced by three key events

THE 1986 ADAMS–KING COMMUNIQUÉ: KEY POINTS

1   What is the nature of the British government's interest in Ireland?
2   What is the British government's attitude toward self-determination, and what will it do to ensure that there is no veto exercised which would militate against the exercise of self-determination?
3   Will the British government play a positive role in persuading unionists toward self-determination?
4   Will the British government publicly state its position, assuming the appropriate replies to these questions?
5   Will the British government accept that the republican movement will represent itself at any negotiations?
6   In the context of dialogue free from interference, will the British government publicly state its intention to withdraw from Ireland and give a date by which such withdrawal will be complete?

King's answer, according to Moloney, set the tone for the British approach well into the 1990s. In his reply King stated:

'But let me be clear! In the second half of the 20th century no matter what has been the position in the past the British government has no political, military, strategic or economic interest in staying in Ireland or in the exercise of authority there that could transcend respect for the wishes of the majority in Northern Ireland'.[12]

in 1987. First, the IRA's hopes of escalating its campaign suffered a setback when the *Eksund*, a freighter carrying significant quantities of ordnance to the IRA, was intercepted and impounded by French authorities. Second, the 'Poppy Day massacre', when a no-warning IRA bomb killed eleven people at a memorial service in Enniskillen, provoked massive public outcry against the movement and threatened to deflect moderate nationalist support away from the republican movement. Third, Sinn Féin published a policy document, *A Scenario for Peace*, which, in the midst of the traditional rhetoric, provided two new 'insights'. These were that dialogue rather than violence might bring about republican objectives, and the hitherto unacknowledged fact that 'unionists existed' in their own right rather than as a deluded section of the Irish people.[14] Building on earlier challenges to republican shibboleths, the Adams project was based on the development of a 'second front'; however, despite the apparently auspicious circumstances, its emergence as the primary Sinn Féin strategy was not guaranteed. Circumstantial evidence points to the conclusion that the advocates of a peace strategy in the republican movement were more ruthless than those who favoured continuing with the armed campaign: for example, questions still remain as to whether the *Eksund* was betrayed by an informant and, more troubling, whether the republican leadership gave the go-ahead in 1990 for the series of human 'proxy bombs' (in which the IRA held families hostage while a loved one was forced to drive vehicle-borne improvised explosive devices into security force buildings and checkpoints) in the knowledge that the strategy would bring opprobrium on the movement. In addition, the Adams project was assisted by the ostracising of potential challengers to his leadership.[15]

Given the uncertainty that existed within the republican movement over its future strategy, it is unsurprising to find that it was also fearful of being outmanoeuvred by the SDLP, which was potentially looking to negotiate with unionists. Thus, during 1988, it argued strongly against power sharing:

> Sinn Féin is totally opposed to a power sharing Stormont assembly and states that there cannot be a partitionist solution.

> Stormont is not a stepping-stone to Irish unity. We believe that
> the SDLP's gradualist theory is therefore invalid and seriously
> flawed.[16]

Despite this, Hume and Adams engaged in a process of secret talks in 1988. Although Hume called off the talks and published the minutes in the *Irish Times* once news of his dialogue with Adams was leaked, the negotiations carried on behind the scenes until the IRA ceasefire of 1994. Arguably, however, the redundancy of the Hume and Adams project was manifest in the fact that he and Adams finally agreed that Britain must become a 'persuader' for Irish unity – implicitly accepting that the SDLP had failed to convince Protestants of the benefits of Irish unification. The neglect of unionist sensibilities was compounded by the decision to pursue a united nationalist front with the Dublin government and the Irish-American lobby in Washington. Indeed, the SDLP again rejected the possibility of power sharing in talks with the Unionist Party in 1992, having been reluctant to see the possibility of the North–South aspects of the Anglo-Irish Agreement being watered down.

Margaret Thatcher resigned from office in 1990 several months after she had appointed Peter Brooke Secretary of State for Northern Ireland. Brooke had broken new ground by making a speech at the University of Ulster, Coleraine, in which he announced, for the first time publicly, that Britain had 'no strategic or economic interest in Northern Ireland'. In reality the end of the Cold War had lessened Britain's obligations under the North Atlantic Treaty Organisation and removed the principal state-based threat to the UK's national security: namely the Soviet Union. Most importantly, Northern Ireland was becoming costly to Britain in terms of blood and treasure. The British government had ensured that the local conflict remained an internal security matter throughout the 1970s and 1980s, despite the cross-currents of state-sponsored terrorism emanating from Colonel Muammar Al-Gaddafi's Libya and the exploits of John Hume and the republican movement in raising the profile of the issue among the higher echelons of Irish America. As Lawrence Freedman observed at the time, the British government had successfully prevented the Northern Ireland conflict from becoming internationalised:

> It is not a regular subject of UN Security Council resolutions, nor the despatch of sundry elder statesmen on mediation missions. London puts much effort into persuading others (in particular American legislators) not to dabble in peace-making, while urging them to deny aid and comfort to the IRA. Keeping the problem defined as one of internal security depends on containing the violence.[17]

Attempts by the Irish government to raise the local dispute at the UN General Assembly were now offset by the closer inter-governmentalism enjoyed during Major's government. Furthermore, the election of Bill Clinton to the office of President of the United States in January 1993 ushered in a new American diplomacy and brought a much-needed fillip to an embryonic peace process.

Initially, republicans remained reticent about engaging with Thatcher's government, although secret 'back-channel' discussions commenced, which continued through until 1994. The collapse of the Soviet Union (1989–91) also served to undermine the republican dogma that Britain enjoyed an imperialistic relationship with Northern Ireland, which provided a vitally important strategic base within the Cold War's balance of power. Furthermore, with the election of Bill Clinton, the United States began more active involvement in Northern Irish politics than had hitherto been the case during the Reagan and Bush years.

Throughout the early 1990s, Hume and Adams continued to

pressure the British government to adopt the position of a 'persuader' for Irish unity. The Downing Street Declaration of December 1993 reaffirmed this position. In what was a tortuously and precisely worded statement the government recognised the nationalist argument for it not to intervene in any future all-Ireland referenda, but also referred to the need to uphold the principle of consent in Northern Ireland:

> The British government agree that it is for the people of the island of Ireland alone, by agreement between the two parts respectively, to exercise their right of self-determination on the basis of consent, freely and concurrently given, North and South, to bring about a united Ireland, if that is their wish.

The IRA began to prepare its membership for a ceasefire by circulating a secret memorandum – the so-called 'TUAS document' – in the summer of 1994. Although the meaning of the acronym was not specified in the paper, it has been taken to mean either 'Totally Unarmed Struggle' or, rather more cynically, 'Tactical Use of Armed Struggle'. The paper argued that an alternative to the armed campaign would create closer alignment between Irish nationalists of different hues – the SDLP, Dublin, and Irish America – and allow Sinn Féin to use that coalition to 'promote basic republican principles'.

This was nothing new: in 1988, for instance, Sinn Féin strategist Tom Hartley argued that republicans should tap into the 'vulnerable green wing' of the SDLP. He claimed that Sinn Féin should concentrate on making 'correct political demands', which the SDLP could not repudiate, but that each time the SDLP agreed, republicans 'should proceed to up the ante by bringing forward new demands'. On the other hand, the TUAS document looked beyond the process of what Hartley called getting 'the SDLP to become more republican' by bringing all nationalist groups under the republican umbrella.[18] The changed international and domestic situation had created new opportunities for Sinn Féin to forward their reunification agenda – or, as the TUAS document stated, 'another front has opened up and we should have the confidence and put in the effort to succeed on that front'. The IRA called a ceasefire at the end of August 1994.

Clinton and US 'soft power'

US support for Irish republicanism had manifested itself throughout the Troubles in the form of financial support and the steady stream of guns and ammunition. Indeed the light, reliable (though no less deadly) Armalite AR-15 rifle first found its way into the hands of IRA volunteers in 1970 via a consignment smuggled into Ireland by a group of republican sympathisers from Philadelphia.[19] Strong support also came from fundraising activities in Irish-American immigrant communities scattered along the East Coast, from Hell's Kitchen in New York, to the pubs of South Boston, and into the board rooms of corporate America. The organisation Irish Northern Aid Committee (NORAID) had been formed as a practical way of channelling money into the hands of the republican movement; it remained a successful enterprise for over thirty years.[20]

However, the Irish-American community also provided a key interest group when it came to the business of peace. The diplomatic wrangling generated by Bill Clinton's decision to grant a forty-eight-hour visa request to Gerry Adams led to a souring of relations between the Clinton and Major administrations in 1994, a veritable low point in the so-called 'Special Relationship'. Clinton's multilateral approach to foreign affairs placed him in the front rank of Democratic presidents, like John

F. Kennedy and Jimmy Carter. Clinton was no less mindful of Carter's record on the Middle East and, indeed, his own orchestration of the handshake on the White House lawn between Yasser Arafat and Yitzhak Rabin was a piece of political theatre, which dampened tensions between Palestinians and Israelis for a few years afterwards.[21]

Republican courtship of the American administration had been indicated clearly in the TUAS document. Provisional republicanism had somersaulted from criticising the US administration to actively supporting it, especially since, with the advent of the Clinton administration, they could profit from a closer association. Indeed one journalist, critical of the Sinn Féin peace strategy, suggests that this new-found cosiness was a deliberate ploy: 'Dumping the anti-American, anti-imperialist chic was part of a plan to use the Americans to politically encircle unionism'.[22] As a further sign of the 'honest broker' stance taken by the US, the Republican Senator for upstate New York George Mitchell was appointed by Clinton as Multi-Party Talks Chairman. This was the high point in the application of American 'soft power', a term employed to describe the process whereby military might plays less of a role in influencing foreign policy goals than the attractiveness of the US economy, culture, beliefs, and values. Against the backdrop of the debacle in Somalia, when United States forces were forced to withdraw following intense gun battles with militants, and the failure to act decisively in Bosnia, the US emerged redeemed on the Northern Ireland conflict, with the 1995 Clinton visit to the province effectively copper-fastening American support for the process.

New Labour and the peace process

New Labour won the British general election in May 1997, ending eighteen years of Conservative Party dominance of

British politics and ushering in a much-needed fresh perspective on the peace process. Prime Minister Tony Blair immediately placed the peace process at the top of his agenda and set about meeting with the various parties to the conflict. Earlier Blair had made several adjustments to Labour's policy on Ireland. Gone was the former spokesman on Northern Ireland Kevin McNamara, who was promptly replaced by the congenial and down-to-earth Mo Mowlam. McNamara had been an unrepentant supporter of Irish unity and was alleged to have been a close associate of the SDLP and Sinn Féin leaderships. He had previously been a leading member of the Troops Out Movement (TOM), a Labour pressure group which had been suing for British military withdrawal since the 1970s. Spearheaded by politicians who would later take up prominent positions in Blair's cabinet (most notably Peter Hain and Clare Short), TOM was marginalised by Blair as he sought to make overtures to Ulster Unionists.

The New Labour leader was particularly concerned about winning over unionist politicians and saw the jettisoning of 'Old' Labour's anti-partitionist stance – and with it the marginalisation of pro-nationalist MPs such as Ken Livingstone and Kevin McNamara – as a necessary first step.[23]

In the run-up to the 1997 election New Labour had indicated a willingness to engage with republicans in a bid to resuscitate an ailing process. Mo Mowlam made several key speeches in which she was unapologetic about Labour's championing of human rights and equality in the past, although she remained sensitive to unionist feelings. Speeches by Blair and Mowlam aimed at encouraging the IRA to renew its ceasefire (which had broken down in February 1996 with a spectacular bombing of the Canary Wharf financial district in London) eventually paid off in July 1997 thereby paving the way for Sinn Féin's reinstatement in the Multi-Party Talks.

The Good Friday Agreement

The signing of the Belfast/Good Friday Agreement represents an unprecedented moment in the history of Anglo-Irish relations. For the first time, the two governments, together with the main representatives of nationalism and unionism in Northern Ireland, agreed to operate a set of political institutions. Although these institutions were based on the different relationships between and within the UK, Ireland, and Northern Ireland, their democratic structures and mechanisms were unique and highly original.

The Agreement was the culmination of a protracted negotiating process and was presented by the SDLP as a vindication of their policies on power sharing and the Irish dimension. Although Sinn Féin had also taken part in the discussions,

THE INSTITUTIONS OF THE GOOD FRIDAY/ BELFAST AGREEMENT

The April 1998 Agreement provided for three sets of institutions: 'Strand One' concerned devolved power sharing in Northern Ireland and the subsequent 108-seat Assembly would be elected by proportional representation and headed by an executive elected according to party strength. 'Strand Two' established the North–South Ministerial Council, whose remit covers a range of socio-economic areas, including tourism, agriculture, and the environment. Finally, 'Strand Three' provided for a British–Irish Council to promote 'harmonious and mutually beneficial' relationships between Britain and Ireland. In addition, the Agreement also provided for the introduction of human rights reforms, the establishment of a commission on police reform, the early release of paramilitary prisoners, and a requirement that all parties use their influence to encourage paramilitary decommissioning.

few commentators or politicians beyond the republican leadership credit its pivotal involvement. Despite the SDLP's central role in the negotiation of the 1998 Agreement, Sinn Féin appeared, to many Northern nationalists, as the more youthful and dynamic party. This was reflected in the political agendas of the two parties – whereas the SDLP attempted to capitalise on what it perceived as a job well done, Sinn Féin continued to emphasise a 'stepping-stone' approach. That approach lay at the heart of Sinn Féin's attempts to sell the Agreement to the broader republican constituency. As Sinn Féin deputy leader, Martin McGuinness, remarked about the Agreement:

> Do we have a level playing field as a result of this phase of negotiations? We clearly do not … it clearly does not go as far as most nationalists and republicans would wish. But it is the basis for advancement.[24]

Gerry Adams also alluded to the idea that the Agreement was only part of a 'phase':

> while the agreement is not a settlement, it is a basis for advancement. It heralds a change in the status quo. And it could become a transitional stage towards reunification but only if all those who express an interest in that objective, especially the powerful and influential, move beyond rhetoric to build a real dynamic for national democratic change.[25]

Arguably, Sinn Féin had no real option other than to portray the Agreement as part of a 'phase', for it represented a repudiation of many of the core aims of the movement. For example, it witnessed the removal of Articles 2 and 3 of the Republic's Constitution, which claimed sovereignty over the North; it instituted recognition of the unionist veto; it locked republicans into partitionist structures and ended their argument that Northern Ireland was an 'illegitimate state' and a 'failed political entity'; finally, it entailed republicans administering British rule in the Six Counties. Understandably, this led one noted political commentator to ask whether 'republicanism [has] finally expired'.[26] Another pointed out that:

> In response to those who argue that the IRA has not been defeated militarily, the obvious answer is that the terrorist group has suffered a clear political defeat since it has failed to achieve any of its objectives.[27]

Ex-activists also struggled to come to terms with the Sinn Féin peace strategy. Former IRA bomber Marian Price maintained:

> They tried to pretend that they had won something when they had won nothing, and they have been pretending ever since. They pretend that walking into Stormont is some sort of achievement. Anybody could have gone out and electioneered and got voted into Stormont in the 1960s. There didn't have to be a war for it.[28]

However, internal political dissent often brings great social and personal costs, such as those witnessed by Brendan Hughes, a former hunger striker and IRA commander and once one of Adams' key allies. Hughes, who suffered from blindness due to his participation in the hunger strikes, was effectively ostracised by Provisional republicans for his opposition to the Adams–McGuinness leadership and for complaints such as:

> I would hate for young people now to have this romanticised version of the events of that time and what went on in the prison, the truth is so very far removed from that and I suppose I'm living proof of that.[29]

Table 1 Electoral change in Northern Ireland (1997–2005)[30]

	Westminster 1997	Westminster 2005	% change
DUP	107,348	241,856	+125
Sinn Féin	126,921	174,530	+37.5
UUP	258,439	127,314	–50.7
SDLP	190,844	125,626	–34.7

In societies that are moving from conflict to peace, myth-making is never politically neutral.[31] That increasing numbers of Northern nationalists have bought into the Sinn Féin 'stepping-stone' narrative is one part of the sea-change in electoral politics over the past decade (see Table 1). The other part – the ramifications of the Sinn Féin mobilisation – is only beginning to be felt. These ramifications relate to the institutionalisation of ethnic experiences and beliefs, and the exclusion of alternative understandings and perspectives on the Troubles, including those based in class or gender relationships. Should that institutionalisation prove to be transitional – given that people's interpretations of the past inevitably change – the problem for Sinn Féin and the current power-sharing détente will switch to how to maintain legitimacy in the face of altered public perceptions and expectations.

For Ulster unionists, the 1998 Agreement entailed several controversial compromises. First, paramilitary prisoners were to be given early release – a provision which was not linked to the decommissioning of paramilitary arms. The Agreement also entailed significant security reforms including a radical overhaul of policing. The former Conservative minister, Chris Patten, headed an inquiry into police reform and published his recommendations in September 1999. The Patten Report avoided the issue of 'lustration' (the removal of officers suspected of rights abuses) but instead proposed that a human rights oath be made part of any new service. Patten also recommended that convicted terrorists be excluded from police recruitment. He went on to suggest that the RUC be renamed and that an office of Police Ombudsman be established. Patten also recommended additional funding for injured RUC officers, and their widows and families. In accordance with the Patten Report, the RUC was renamed the Police Service of Northern Ireland (PSNI) and an Ombudsman was appointed in November 2000. Many unionists interpreted these changes not only as favouring nationalism to the detriment of unionism but also believed that the changes were an affront to their beliefs about the Troubles: thus, the IRA was being rewarded with early release and seats for their politicians in government while the security forces who had defended law and order were restructured. 'Reform', in this perspective, seemed to imply that the police were culpable for the violence, and republicans the innocent victims.

The 1998 Agreement, therefore, set in motion renewed political contestation over who was right and who was wrong about the past – a debate that involved fundamental questions about how people viewed themselves and each other, and how they explained their beliefs. Because this debate involved such fundamental questions about identities, the Agreement helped to initiate a renewed period of electoral polarisation as voters flocked to the political extremes.

Conclusion

The Good Friday Agreement did not automatically settle the conflict in Northern Ireland, nor did it lead to the permanent eradication of physical violence, intimidation, and conflict within or between communities. Paramilitaries had long policed the interface areas in which Protestant and Catholic housing estates converged and in which they had grass-roots support throughout their long and bloody campaigns of violence. Community representatives close to the military wings of nationalism and unionism freely admit that the paramilitaries could simply turn violence on and off like a tap and the Agreement changed little. In 2001–2 rioting in Belfast was at the same level as it had been twenty years before. Images of children caught in the cross-fire between rival loyalist and republican communities in many ways embodied the depth of division in the midst of jubilant scenes of handshaking and backslapping between politicians. Less evident was how the vacuum created by political stalemate did not lead to a return to open sectarian conflict.

5

Institutional stalemate and community relations, 1998–2008

'Civil society' in Northern Ireland

The 1998 Good Friday Agreement did not automatically lead to the dissipation of sectarian conflict. Instead, community relations (CR) workers became instrumental in stabilising the peace process at a time when the political process became stalemated. Politically, the advent of New Labour in 1997 signalled a much-needed impetus to an ailing peace process while also introducing a new discourse of 'community relations'. By 2008 the community and voluntary sector employed over 29,000 paid workers in Northern Ireland,[1] employment figures on a par with the glory days of the shipbuilding industry in the 1960s. Since 1997 the sector has enjoyed over £2 billion of funding from Europe, as well as almost £1 billion in other grants from a range of government and charitable sources. The growth in the so-called 'peace business' has not always been welcomed. It could be argued that it led to a dependency on grant-awarding funding bodies and a narrow perspective on hurriedly trans-forming the local conflict beyond violence overnight, an impossible mission in a society gripped by sectarian violence for over a generation. This has led to what one experienced voluntary sector worker has called 'short-termism', a mentality which hinges on the prospect of further bridging funding to continue with community relations work.[2] Peacebuilding theorist John Paul Lederach has articulated the need to move beyond this '"project mentality" (1–3 years maximum) to a

THE COMMUNITY RELATIONS FIELD

Community relations work grew out of community development and housing association projects in the 1970s, which became involved in lobbying central government for urban regeneration and slum clearance. In its current guise the community relations field dates from the early 1990s when a number of projects sprouted up in those areas where violent conflict had been at its most pronounced. So-called 'interface areas', where Protestants and Catholics continue to live uneasily side by side, were targeted by government grants and charitable organisations as being those most in need of aid. The intermediary agencies through which such 'capacity' was built included funding bodies such as the Community Relations Council and the Community Foundation for Northern Ireland. Various community-based organisations (CBOs) were established and sought competitive funding for various projects in local areas. CR workers became the main points of contact 'on the ground'. The conflict resolution expert John Paul Lederach credits CR workers with aiding in the transformation of the Northern Ireland conflict, particularly in those areas where sectarian violence has been endemic. In his words, 'the single most important aspect that made the processes of transformation stick and overcome considerable obstacles in the 1990s–2000s as opposed to similar efforts that collapsed at various points in the earlier three decades is found in the community-based webs of people, relationships, and activities that were not nearly so robustly present in earlier timeframes. Local communities and the cross-stitching of communities represents a central, if not the key aspect to sustaining constructive change.'[3]

decade capacity when thinking and planning for change'. He maintains that the complexities of change in deep-rooted conflicts mean that practitioners, donors, and the wider public must recalibrate their thinking on such matters.[4] Lederach's thinking on peace processes has won many admirers among CR workers in Northern Ireland.

For decades community cohesion was disrupted by the activities of loyalist and republican paramilitary groups, who fought a seemingly endless campaign of violence in areas with a perceived weak community infrastructure. Much of the violence occurred in working-class areas of Belfast and Derry/Londonderry, and the rural hamlets of South Armagh, Mid Ulster, and East Tyrone; the bulk of the deaths can be plotted according to similar demographics. Despite this inauspicious environment the community/voluntary sector developed in the shadow of elite-level politics, coming more to the forefront since signing of the Good Friday Agreement in 1998.

Moreover, the benefit of community-based initiatives to peacebuilding in Northern Ireland was recognised and incorporated into the Good Friday Agreement. Under Article 13 of the Rights, Safeguards and Opportunities component:

> The participants recognise and value the work being done by many organisations to develop reconciliation and mutual understanding and respect between and within communities and traditions, in Northern Ireland and between North and South, and they see such work as having a vital role in consolidating peace and political agreement. Accordingly, they pledge their continuing support to such organisations and will positively examine the case for enhanced financial assistance for the work of reconciliation. An essential aspect of the reconciliation process is the promotion of a culture of tolerance at every level of society, including initiatives to facilitate and encourage integrated education and mixed housing.[5]

Low-level British government sponsorship of integrated education programmes signalled a commitment to tackling one aspect of structural sectarianism, but it fell to the European Union, the International Fund for Ireland, and a host of other American and European grant-awarding bodies to plug the gaps created by central British government funding for other community-based projects.

Despite the enormous difficulties of the peacebuilding tasks envisioned in the Belfast Agreement, there was something of a disparity in government-level rhetoric and actually dealing with the transition from war to peace. The difficult and dangerous task of post-conflict reconstruction was left to CR workers, aided in their capacity-building activities by other non-governmental organisations (NGOs) and community-based organisations (CBOs). Most CR workers are reluctant to take credit for the work they have undertaken and instead leave it to those who played supporting roles (often middle-class professionals and politicians geographically removed from the sharp end of conflict) to accept plaudits on their behalf. Occasionally, some CR practitioners are prepared to be a little more explicit about their role in peace-building:

> I believe that 'what price is peace'. I believe that if it hadn't have been for the work of community relations workers we would not have got the conflict transformed; so let's not think that the politicians did all the work here, because they didn't. A lot of community workers (on the ground) were part and parcel of bringing about the ceasefire, as were some of the key named stakeholders in the conflict. And, if it hadn't been for community relations work, I don't think the energy would have been there for the ceasefire to happen, because I do believe that community relations work did help.[6]

In most accounts of the immediate post-Agreement years the community/voluntary sector is rarely afforded due recognition for its successes in tackling sectarianism in interface areas. Neil Jarman observes how:

> In many ways the peace had to be built from the bottom up as much as from the top down and this process involved diverse groups, organisations and activities, and included managing tensions and disorder on the ground and building relationships with erstwhile enemies and opponents.[7]

Incredibly, many former paramilitaries who had once trained their weapons' sights on each other now sought to work together on cross-community projects to challenge sectarianism on the interfaces, for the betterment of their respective communities. This was not always welcomed – sometimes it led to further distrust and entrenchment, while at other times it had a positive effect of breaking down stereotypes.

For CR practitioners in Protestant/unionist/loyalist communities across Belfast, the violence was an inbuilt fault of the peace process itself, which had led to a de-escalation of the military dimension of the conflict but not a solution to the problem:

> Yes, ok, it's great to see peace. But it's a truce. For me there's a difference there between a truce, peace and equality, and all that sort of related stuff. A truce is to say, 'OK, we won't use violence, but we'll live in our own communities and be divided as we were, without the violence.'[8]

There is a palpable feeling shared by practitioners in both communities that the end of military conflict left a huge vacuum that might be exploited by those ultra-republican and -loyalist groupings that wished to pursue a rejectionist path. 'Spoiler groups' remain the principal threats to the peace process in Northern Ireland in the absence of purposeful peace and reconciliation.[9]

The need for reconciliation often follows in the wake of protracted inter-community conflicts, especially those with an ethnic dimension. Yet in Northern Ireland, despite the symbolism of former arch-enemies entering into government, there has been a lack of open reconciliation. Indeed, very little has been done to tackle the difficult task of rebuilding a broken society. Instead, internecine feuding, inter-community disturbances, and animosity between and within communities have remained a constant feature of much of post-Agreement society.

The Belfast Agreement and interface violence

The number of recorded violent incidents along what became known as 'interface areas' did not dissipate after the signing of the Belfast Agreement. Indeed, if anything, violence increased as the two communities interpreted the Agreement as giving ground to the other side. In a zero–sum conflict (i.e. where one side is perceived to have 'won', while the other side is perceived to have 'lost') like Northern Ireland, the traditional thinking of winning and losing retained much of its potency and dictated the course of action during relative peace. Many observers hoped that the evolution of 'civil society' would offset sectarian competition and conflict, but instead the Belfast Agreement simply reinforced the dominant ethnically exclusivist nature of the governing institutions at Stormont. In Irish history one side had to be beaten and the zero–sum nature of the ethno-nationalist conflict meant that events and episodes had to be simplistically reduced to a dichotomous black and white picture.

Moreover, the Belfast Agreement did not automatically lead to a reduction in sectarian tensions between communities in either of the province's two main cities, Belfast and Derry/Londonderry, either. Despite the outward appearance of peace and reconciliation, nothing could be further from the

POLICE REFORM: FROM RUC TO PSNI

The RUC was formed on 1 June 1922 and officially rebranded as the Police Service of Northern Ireland in November 2001 under proposals put forward by the Patten Commission on policing in the province. The Patten proposals (1999) promised the rebranding of the RUC as a community police service and included reduction in size, 50/50 Protestant/Catholic recruitment, the removal of the Oath of Allegiance to the Queen, and neutral symbols, among other recommendations. Three hundred and two RUC officers lost their lives during the conflict. Her Majesty Queen Elizabeth II awarded the RUC the George Cross on 12 April 2000 in recognition of its bravery in dealing with the terrorist threat.

reality on the ground. As one respected community representative in the Waterside area of Londonderry remarked:

> From the signing of the Good Friday Agreement everyone thought 'yep, peace at last in Northern Ireland'. They looked at the aspect of no more killings, no more bombings ... I personally fully supported that. But on the issue of sectarianism [between] the two communities, ten years later, are as far apart as ever. There are people here in Londonderry who will deny that sectarianism exists ... [and demonstrate this by pointing to] good community relationships and good citizenship programmes and protocols that are operating through the schools. And when you look at sectarianism in the interface areas ... it's there, it's not going away. People are in denial.[10]

Other Belfast-based CR workers make similar observations, rejecting the idea that violence at the interfaces can be dismissed simply as 'anti-social behaviour', a term used principally by the PSNI and local government bodies to explain the persistence of interface trouble:

> Anti-social behaviour … if it's between the different communities, say it be loyalist or republican, as we have seen … in the New Lodge and … elements from the Shankill, or whatever, where there have been clashes and people have put that down to anti-social behaviour. I don't think it is: I think it is sectarianism full-stop. But it's dressed over to say it's anti-social for those who say that 'Yes, we are containing this here.' I believe that, whether we would have had the Troubles or not, there would have been a certain amount of anti-social behaviour anyway, but I think it's wrong to dress it up and sort of smooth over the cracks that still remain in this whole process.[11]

The undercurrent of deep-seated hatred and animosity continued to flow through interface areas even after the Good Friday Agreement was signed. One of the consequences of the stalemate engendered by the local institutions was a descent into violence between loyalist paramilitaries. The two main organisations, the UDA and the UVF, had issued a joint ceasefire statement on 13 October 1994; however, the lack of discipline among members of these organisations led to a tendency to settle local differences, personality clashes, and old scores by internecine feuding. The formation of the Loyalist Volunteer Force (LVF) in 1996 by the former Mid Ulster UVF commander Billy Wright was a rejection of the UVF's military policy of temporarily suspending its campaign of armed resistance.

There was nothing pre-ordained about the departure of the LVF from the UVF fold. According to the overall leader of the UVF, Wright burst into tears when the ceasefire was announced and declared that he would be ditching his gloves and balaclava for pen and paper at university. Wright's plans were put on hold after he and his followers publicly opposed what he termed the Progressive Unionist Party's (PUP) brand of 'compromise politics'. The expulsion of Wright and his unit from the UVF, and the subsequent discovery of an unsuccessful assassination plot against him by fellow loyalists, led to a huge rally in Portadown at which the sitting Mid Ulster DUP MP William McCrea spoke out in support of Wright. The LVF continued to remain a thorn in the side of the UVF, even after Wright's assassination in the Maze prison at the hands of Irish National Liberation Army (INLA) prisoners in December 1997.

By 2000 the complex conflict within loyalism reached boiling point and the unfurling of LVF colours outside the Rex Bar in the Shankill provoked a violent response from the UVF. UDA godfather Johnny 'Mad Dog' Adair gave military protection to the LVF and chose to lead his notorious C Company unit into direct conflict with the UVF. By the end of the feud

LOYALIST POLITICS: THE PROGRESSIVE UNIONIST PARTY

The PUP was formed in 1979. It is one of the smallest parties in Northern Ireland, in terms of both membership size and share of the vote. Propelled into the media spotlight by the loyalist ceasefires in 1994, the PUP won two seats in the first elections to the Northern Ireland Assembly in 1998 although, it commanded only 0.6% of the vote in the March 2007 Northern Ireland Assembly election. The PUP is unique in that it boasts a democratic socialist ideology and working class character. Despite having a firm grounding of support in the Protestant working-class community, the PUP seeks to empower all working-class communities in the province. Its first leader was Hugh Smyth, one of the longest-serving members of Belfast City Council. Former UVF prisoner David Ervine became its leader from 2002 until his death in January 2007. Ervine was one of the most well-known and most articulate politicians in Northern Ireland. The current leader is Dawn Purvis, who was re-elected to Ervine's seat in the East Belfast constituency in March 2007.

seven men lay dead, including one PUP member in his sixties, as a direct result of his alleged involvement in the killing of a UDA member in the 1970s. Another low-ranking UVF member from Rathcoole on the outskirts of North Belfast was shot several times in the head at point-blank range; the fleeing gunmen were heard chanting 'up the T'Bay UDA' by local children as they made their escape. Adair had been seen a few days earlier at the Rathcoole's Tuesday morning market outside the UDA headquarters in the estate and just yards from where UVF member Mark Quail was later gunned down. Adair remained a destabilising influence in loyalism until he was expelled by the UDA/UFF in 2002.

The tense atmosphere across loyalist areas in Northern Ireland was palpable. As one careful observer of loyalism put it: 'The concentrated ferocity of this cycle of Loyalist killing simply added to North Belfast's existing problems, but that [t]here was hope, too, in the fact that, as in August, the UDA as a whole was not involved in the ongoing violence.'[12] There were even signs that the UVF had not brought its destructive capabilities to bear in vicious reprisals, partly as a consequence of the calming influence exerted by several high-profile PUP activists and CR workers. On 22 November a joint UDA–UVF statement announced an end of the infighting.[13]

The effects of internecine feuding on Ulster loyalism were far reaching. Not only did these actions divide the loyalist community further, they also adversely affected the way in which loyalists were perceived by the outside world. Moreover, nationalists and republicans feared that the feud would spill over into violence on their community. This was certainly the case in that the undercurrent of sectarianism became the logical expression of pathological tendencies among some young loyalists. The catalogue of murders in the North Belfast and Antrim areas of young Catholics Daniel McColgan (aged twenty), Gerard Lawlor (aged nineteen) and Ciaran Cummings (aged nineteen), left deep emotional scars in the tight-knit working-class communities of North Belfast. Another young man, Gavin Brett, a Protestant, had been fatally wounded the year before in a drive-by shooting. Several of the gunmen came from the Newtownabbey area, a predominantly Protestant borough on the outskirts of North Belfast.

Hyped up on sectarianism and drunk on an inflated sense of superiority, the perpetrators of these murders were also young men groomed by older paramilitaries who remained disgruntled by the peace process. Responding to community-based calls for security, republican gunmen shot and wounded a young Protestant man in Ardoyne. Unrelated to the tit-for-tat violence in Belfast, dissident republicans murdered a former soldier as he carried out repairs on a British (Territorial) Army base in Londonderry. The escalation in murders, inter-communal street disturbances, and attacks on churches saw thousands of people gather outside Belfast City Hall for a massive anti-sectarian rally in the summer of 2002. Addressing the rally, Irish Congress of Trade Unions representative Bob Gourley denounced the ongoing violence and urged paramilitary groups to dissolve:

> Sectarianism kills and paramilitary groups have not offered freedom, justice, equality or security, but only an ever-spiralling decline into economic and social deprivation, loss of jobs and the growth of anti-social behaviour.[14]

Politicians and government officials were quick to condemn the upsurge in sectarianism, but it was CR workers who recognised that many of these attacks were perpetrated without recourse to religious piety. In 2002 community relations reached an all-time low when a Provisional IRA spy-ring was uncovered at Stormont. The Secretary of State Peter Mandelson immediately suspended the Assembly, leaving a political stalemate that mirrored frustration and angst at street-level.

These incidents were the product of a naked sectarianism

that was something of a slow-burning fuse among many young men in loyalist and republican areas. For one former loyalist prisoner, the feeling was that the peace process had not delivered and was fuelling fear, uncertainty, and violence:

> I never, ever assumed that the leadership of the paramilitaries would say 'let's have peace'. That has to filter down to the ground and people on the ground have to see the benefits and rewards of that. And I don't think there's been any benefits, certainly for the loyalist community (and that's in my opinion), through this peace process. Yes, the killing has stopped and that's good for everybody. But in terms of social and economic benefits: where are they?[15]

In Derry City some community workers have pointed to the absence of the Protestant community in the day-to-day management of the peace process:

> In some ways the Protestant community has taken its eye off the ball in community relations ... The biggest minority community in the city was never mentioned [at public meetings about minority rights]. We are still here and we haven't gone away.[16]

Many grass-roots unionists became despondent and apathetic towards the peace process yet, for republicans, an even greater chasm would soon open and threaten to derail the Sinn Féin peace strategy.

The republican movement (the Provisional IRA and Sinn Féin) were able to maintain cohesion and discipline in their ranks because they were less diffuse and more centrally controlled than loyalists. In the words of disgruntled former member Anthony McIntyre they imposed a kind of 'newspeak', 'an environment where those disgruntled with the Belfast Agreement are repeatedly told, in Orwellian fashion, that the "Peace Process is watching you".' In the post-Good Friday

Agreement era this meant that for republicans, in McIntyre's view, 'The IRA definitely had not gone away. Rather, the party was to be ruled with the ethos of the army.'[17] This was to be regretted, in the view of some critics, as Irish republicanism sought out more 'authoritarian methods of internal control'.[18] Republicans embittered by the Provisional project have also noted the futility of the 'armed struggle' in that it was fought for little reward:

> The merest hint of dissent infuriates it by publicly reminding it, in spite of its narcissism, of how little is actually achieved in return for all the people it both put to and sent to their deaths.[19]

In McIntyre's opinion the British state's 'strategic objective' in supporting the Good Friday Agreement was 'to include Republicans while excluding republicanism'.[20] This caused problems for the Provisional IRA, which had by now invested its faith in the logic of the Belfast Agreement and the belief that demographic change would favour a united Ireland some time in the future.[21] Sinn Féin's official line, though, was bound up in the knowledge that it is now in responsible government. However, while republicans close to the organisation may have bought into the process, according to critics like McIntyre and Bean, that does not detract from the problems this has created on the ground. For instance, CR workers in North Belfast were being increasingly told after 2005 that the IRA had 'gone away' and that they must deal with anti-social behaviour in conjunction with local agencies and the PSNI.

'It's good to talk': the impact of cross-community dialogue

The community relations field in Northern Ireland has been operating largely under the political radar since 1998. The dynamics of interface violence did alter, however, as the military dimension of the conflict began to wind down. Begrudgingly, paramilitaries loosened their grip on territory, and punishment beatings and other forms of social control dissipated. Nevertheless, there still remained challenges, as one CR worker recalled:

Well since the calm down of Drumcree, interface violence has – people don't view it as serious as it used to be, but it has always the potential [to spill over] so you can't rest on your laurels. Really you can't sit back and say 'right we're in a relative peace now, that's it'. We need to maintain our contacts, and we need to maintain the Mobile Phone Network. The importance of it is still there, because sectarianism hasn't gone away. If anything sectarianism in young people is different from the sectarianism we had – in all of us – whenever we were growing up during the Troubles because there was a reason for it. The reason has seemed to go away, yet the sectarianism and the hatred, that's there. You can see it in the young people. I mean two weeks ago at Lundy's parade – like what reason do young nationalists and young unionists have to roar abuse at one another across [the divide], you know. Yet they still do it.[22]

Violence at the interfaces in Derry/Londonderry has certainly dissipated since the signing of the Agreement. Yet sectarian incidents have not gone away. PSNI figures reveal that 282 incidents were recorded between April 2006 and April 2007 in the main interface areas of Bishop Street/Fountain, Irish Street/Gobnascale and Tullyally/Currynieran.[23] Such violence has created an uneasy impasse, according to some CR workers:

I think the normal conditions are that people are in their comfort zone and people are quite content with the level of conflict that we have because it is less violent. We're content not to meet the other side because to meet the other side means that you might be giving something.[24]

Of these 282 incidents 120 were reported in the Bishop Street/Fountain area, a troublespot which sees a small team of nationalist/republican residents working single-handedly and voluntarily to de-escalate the conflict on a nightly, all-year-round basis.

New Labour's policy on community relations has played a crucial role in shaping the methodology of community relations work. Peacebuilding jargon has become a standard component of republican and loyalist peacebuilding activities. As one senior community relations worker from the PUL community in the Waterside area of Derry/Londonderry pointed out:

> We had a stage where we had families living with suitcases packed and kids sleeping under kitchen tables because the front of their houses were being constantly attacked. Now, you nearly watched the news 24/7 just for the fear of something [happening] because if it sparked off in Belfast, well if it was a loyalist uprising, the first place it happened, it would have been Tullyally; where if it was a nationalist uprising it would have been the Bogside. Donnacha McNellis [a nationalist community leader] said to me one time 'It's either us or youse', you know. So you were always watching for that spark – that it could manifest itself in your own community. And people just lived on their nerves. I don't see that any more. I see people, I suppose, through an influx of funding and business creation, I see our community being more open for people in the other community. It's still a loyalist community but with the new shopping precinct there's a lot of footfall from people from the other community. There's a lot of inter-mixing that there would not have been before the Troubles. It's not so easy to fight with someone that you know, or that you're getting to know in the street.[25]

Undoubtedly the conflict mediation role played by CR practitioners (often for little or no reward) led to a huge decrease in sectarian tensions at the main interfaces in Derry City, with the Bishop Street/Fountain interface seeing a sixty-one per cent drop in the twelve months leading up to February 2008.[26] However, as many mediators would freely admit, it has by no means eradicated it altogether. The question must be asked, then: why does sectarianism persist and how can it be tackled at its root?

Sectarianism: ignoring the elephant in the room?

There is almost a universal impression that the conflict in Northern Ireland is over and that, the sudden proliferation of construction cranes, new buildings and economic prosperity in the years after 1998 signalled an end of the conflict. Behind the facade of multi-million-pound housing developments, apartment blocks, and plush landscaped gardens, sectarianism remains rife. The influx of new migrant communities from eastern Europe has added a potential new security problem for the PSNI, who define sectarian, racist, and homophobic attacks as 'hate crime'. In the words of one experienced CR worker in North Belfast:

> For me, as far as I'm concerned, sectarianism is as rife now as it was pre-ceasefires. If anything, it's got worse – people are more entrenched within their local communities. I suppose in one sense what you have now is the explanation for sectarianism, which in my view still is – as [a form of] anti-social behaviour: rioting. We've got to ask the question: who does that suit to say that and to put it off that way? My view is, and remains, that we still live in a very sectarian country. In terms of how do we deal with that, I suppose in one sense it is true to say that 'yes', we did try to fill a vacuum whenever politics just wasn't

working – until the institutions got up and running. In many senses we led the way as community workers. Politicians, I wouldn't say took over from what we did (they don't) but took our lead. And, I suppose in one sense, it was a benchmark as to where they could start to work for themselves and I suppose we were the sound-bites for them.[27]

Among a sizable number of conflict mediation practitioners there is a cynicism about the nature of the Agreement and the role of politicians in selling its benefits to people living in close proximity to 'the other' community:

So, at the end of the day, the bottom line is, sectarianism is so rife today, not just here in Londonderry – right across Northern Ireland. Ballymena is a prime example; I'm involved in a project up there – sectarianism is so, so rife.[28]

The on-the-ground reality of enduring enmities in Northern Ireland points towards the residual unfinished business of the so-called 'Troubles'.

So is there actually peace and reconciliation in Northern Ireland? It is often quite difficult to gauge the true extent to which both communities have moved closer together, especially in a society that has been segregated for generations and where people of different ethnic, religious, and national identity leanings sometimes live within yards of one another but with little experience of their neighbours. Much heat has been generated from middle-class professionals about the need to resolve ancient enmities and move forward together to a more peaceful future. Yet much of the writing on 'dealing with the past' neglects to discuss the elephant in the room, which is that the Belfast Agreement is a model for *managing* conflict between Protestant Unionists and Catholic Nationalists, not *resolving* it. There is no sense in which the conflict will wither away. Thus, many commentators approach the debate from an idealist perspective when in actual fact they should do so from a viewpoint grounded in realism. As the academic Kevin Bean has perceptively argued:

> In the polarized politics and segregated society of Northern Ireland, the Provisionals' new language of reconciliation was just another way of strengthening their electoral support and pursuing the old struggle for communal advantage.[29]

No wonder Protestants remain sceptical about the peace process. In a society deeply divided along ethnic lines the past will never properly be dealt with when it is used to justify a present or future political position.[30] By rewriting the past to justify their actions Sinn Féin and the DUP have attempted to sanitise the past in ways that may lead to inaccurate understandings of what took place during the conflict and could potentially lead to a resurgence of tension in the future.

Moreover, there is also the feeling among many CR workers that economic resources have always constrained the impact CBOs can make on conflict in the region. Michael Doherty, a CR practitioner in Derry City, maintains that:

> But, unfortunately, we got a pittance. We had to depend on money coming from Europe. Where were the incentives coming from the British government – or the Irish government – who gave us absolutely nothing in relation to what came in from Europe? Because what was given to the Community Relations Council from the Central Community Relations Unit was hardly £2 a head, per capita, per year, so when people talk about the millions of pounds – it came from Europe. And if it hadn't have been for European money I don't know what we would have done. And not only do we need [it], I reckon we need millions and millions more pounds ... to work us over the next generation to keep another life [and] from keeping somebody else from getting killed here.[31]

In reality few people wish to talk about what happened in the past because it is still raw and contemporaneous. There is an old adage in Northern Ireland that sectarianism and the pain inflicted by one community on another community is like the proverbial 'elephant in the room'. As one CR worker suggested:

> What we are doing here is we are actually ignoring the elephant that's in the room along with us … [W]hile I agree we have transformed the conflict … I believe that in another ten or fifteen years we could be back in the circle again [if we don't continue to address sectarianism and the past] if the 'No' campers decide to have another go at trying to unify Ireland or reinforce Britishness within the Six County context. So, I mean somebody said to me I'm a bit of a pessimist in all of this and I'm saying no I think I'm a realist. Because I have been looking at and studying conflict, and the dynamics of conflict, and we're running the danger that if we don't keep putting money into this kind of work, we are going to get complacent again and we are going to allow our young people to go round the circle [of conflict again].[32]

The serious repercussions of sectarianism have been far reaching in Northern Ireland and the main focus of community relations training and education has been on challenging stereotypes and false perceptions. Re-inserting the human dimension back into community engagement has been the main focus of not only intermediatory funding bodies such as the Community Relations Council and the Community Foundation for Northern Ireland, but also the thousands of groups that have received funding since the mid to late 1990s. In many ways, the critique that too much money has been channelled into these groups holds little water. Not only has it been measured in terms of the relative peace which has bedded down in recent years but it has certainly cost the tax-payer a lot less than the alternative security bill that would be run up in the event of a slide back into all-out military conflict.

Dealing with the past: old wine in new bottles?

In Northern Ireland the reluctance on the part of both communities to forgive and forget meant that the Agreement could not have the far-reaching effect that most of the outside world expected of it. The local conflict remains unique in that the military dimension of the conflict has wound down quite significantly since 1994 and been successfully transformed beyond violence. In large part this was due to the willingness on all sides to compromise and to the fact that the conflict, however bloody and protracted it seemed, had limited political goals at stake for all sides. Only in South Africa, in a process which resulted in the wholesale abolition of the existing state, did the path towards democracy run as smoothly. The predominance of separatism, ethnic conflict, and insurgency in Israel–Palestine, the Basque region, and Sri Lanka are perhaps more typical of the prolonged nature of contemporary violence.

The idea that conflicts in deeply divided societies move seamlessly from conflict to peace and on to reconciliation is an idealist myth, propagated by those with vested interests. There is no instance in the world today where two rival ethnic groups have come together to live in harmony with each other. And this is reflected in those areas where violence has been most acute during the Troubles. One CR worker revealed how tense relationships between the two communities still remained:

> Mediation-wise, you know, incidents do happen – still happen – on interfaces. I suppose in one sense, if you look at sectarianism and racism [they] are loaded guns with different triggers and I suppose it depends on where people live as to what causes those. It could be to do with housing. I suppose in one sense it's about dialogue, but I don't think that we've got to the stage,

at the community level, where we can talk about the hard
issues, the issues that matter to people. I suppose it's easy to put
a blanket over something and say, 'Yes, that's a sectarian issue',
but what triggers those issues? And people aren't talking.[33]

The above quote reveals how difficult and complex conflict
actually remains in Northern Ireland, even with a significant
drop in violent incidents in the region. Other projects
involving former paramilitaries and prisoners reached out
across the divide by refocusing the efforts of CR workers
towards practical conflict management and reduction activities.
One well-respected community worker from West Belfast,
Harry Donaghy, when asked why he remained committed to
peacebuilding work, remarked:

Personally, [it is] as a natural outcome of all of that interrelated
[community relations] work. Whether it be with the ex-
prisoner groups over a long number of years now, or the more
challenging cross-community engagement projects, and the
general theme of reconciliation and peacebuilding. I think it's
very, very important that these topics or issues aren't quietly put
away to the sidelines, when people do have a habit of, [saying],
well, 'We actually won't talk about the war', or 'We won't talk
about contentious subjects such as [this or] that'. It's fundamental if we are to have, in the years to come – for generations
to come – what's called 'a shared future' or 'a better future', or
whatever the terminology; then we have to become, as people,
comfortable with the whole concept of identity, and allegiance,
and difference. It has to be the building block of a new understanding of historical differences between unionism and nationalism, or loyalism and republicanism. We have to agree on the
conditions, where we as a society and a people are comfortable
with the concepts of British and Irish identities, and how
we can accommodate one another in whatever structures are
agreed on for the future.[34]

Conclusion

While the military dimension has certainly been in a process of de-escalation since the mid 1990s there is still a considerable amount of animosity and hatred detectable within and between communities. This is a daily reality encountered by those who have vowed to rebuild a better society after decades of armed conflict in Northern Ireland. As one experienced conflict mediator pointed out:

> Nobody wants to go back to those dark days. I don't think there's anybody and I think there'd be a lot of people in the communities that would stop it or do their utmost to stop it. But the potential threat's always there. And that's what we're hearing day and daily ... Sectarianism is there to an extent – but I don't know if it's that deep that it would encourage someone to go out and murder or shoot or plant a bomb. It's a different type of sectarianism nearly ... We are actually working out the effects of the Troubles now.[35]

This is a view shared by other CR workers in Londonderry, who lay much of the blame for the continuing violence at the door of the political establishment in the province:

> The politicians – the good and great and wonderful people, as I would refer to them – who would maintain that they are there in the coalface areas. They're not there. People like myself and my colleagues, be it from the Protestant community or the nationalist community, are there till three, four, five in the morning. And also, I must say, the clergy. There is no involvement from the clergy. I have already spoken to a few of the clergy and they would like to get involved, but when it comes to getting their hands dirty I'm afraid, you know, the bottom line is nobody wants to know. PSNI: their resources are dwindling. They have the strength of what? 7500. By 2010/11

it's going to be reduced to between 5000 and 6000. Police in the town will admit they don't have the manpower ... So when violence escalates community police officers are not properly equipped to deal with it so they rely on the community representatives to sort it out.[36]

Developments in Northern Ireland in March 2009 have shown that politicians are capable of responding to the groundswell of opinion for cross-community unity in the face of the threat posed by dissident Irish republicans. Determined not to weaken the process which they helped to construct from the 'bottom-up', CR workers, trade unionists, and ordinary people rallied against the acts perpetrated by those who wished to drag the province back on to a war-footing. The general consensus is that conflict should not be allowed to return to the province and that, invariably, the killings in 2009 served as an adhesive binding the new institutions together. This is in complete contrast to previous generations, where violence has been a destabilising factor in edging Northern Ireland ever closer to conflict. Yet, all levels of society have made that possible, from the politicians, to the clergy, academics, and funding agencies, to those CR workers at the grass roots. The remarkable drive towards preventing further retrenchment is one of the distinguishing features of the latent stages of the Northern Ireland conflict.

6

'An age-old problem'. Why did the Troubles happen?

Explaining Northern Ireland

The Northern Ireland conflict is often explained by reference to two opposing 'sides' – primordial entities usually designated as either 'Protestant–Catholic', 'Unionist–Nationalist', or 'British–Irish'. In turn, these pairings imply a tacit understanding that the Northern Ireland conflict was primarily to do with (a) religious differences, (b) inter-communal or ideological divisions, (c) nationalist antagonism, or (d) some combination. Although scholars continue to disagree over where the emphasis should be placed, there is common agreement that the presence of two communities, with different allegiances and political aspirations, is central to the 'Northern Ireland problem'. Yet while this core fact is largely beyond dispute, it doesn't actually tell us why there was a problem. In other words, pointing out the presence of two communal blocs or 'traditions' merely *describes* the most prominent feature of the conflict; it does not *explain* what the conflict was about, why it erupted when it did, why it persisted for so long, or why the violence came to an end.

Thinking about the Northern Ireland conflict in terms of competing and antagonistic conceptions of national belonging does not differ significantly from the traditional communal resort to blaming the other side. The logic is essentially the same: a group of people – defined on the basis of reputed religious, political, or cultural similarities – acted in such and such a way simply because they believed in the same set of values or shared the same characteristics.

By taking as the starting point for any explanation the idea that the conflict was somehow inevitable due to the presence of antagonistic communities leads inevitably to looking only for those things that support the initial idea. Alternative facts, stories, and experiences are neglected, and those voices that were marginalised by the violence remain silenced in the peace. While it is reasonable to assume that antagonistic politics creates a rippling, tit-for-tat effect, this does not tell the whole story of the Northern Ireland conflict. In this case there is nothing inevitable about conflict. Choices are made and alternatives declined – not simply because of irreconcilable ideologies but often on the basis of the fragmentary or biased lessons people learned about their past experiences.

It is important to dissect these assumptions because they provide a framework for particular stories people tell about the conflict and provide barriers to others. In other words, these assumptions are intensely value laden. While this may not in itself be a bad thing, the problem – as outlined in greater detail in the conclusion – is that the deliberate or unquestioned exclusion of particular points of view only serves to postpone any hoped-for conflict resolution.[1]

The ethnic conflict model

Many people, both in the scholarly community and in Northern Ireland itself, see the Troubles as having involved a combination of conflicts. Thus, the conflict involved not only two distinct religious factions – Catholics and Protestants – but also two distinct historical communities and two distinct visions for the future. Coupled with this was the presence of two different 'homeland' states that each community looked to for support and identified with. The idea that the Troubles were not caused solely by unionist obduracy or nationalists wishing to end partition, but by a combination of factors involving groupings within and outside Northern Ireland has come to be known as the 'ethnic conflict model'.[2] This catch-all title describes the different ways in which the people of Northern Ireland identify themselves: communally (nationalist–unionist), religiously (Catholic–Protestant), or nationally (British–Irish). It also takes into account the idea that there are wider dimensions to the Northern Ireland conflict: in the first instance, the role of the British and Irish states, and, second, the influence exerted by international actors such as the European Union and the United States.

The ethnic conflict model is, therefore, simply a way of thinking about the Troubles. According to the model, antagonistic identities reinforce each other. Thus, Protestants tend to vote for unionist parties and aspire to be part of the UK, whereas Catholics tend to vote for nationalist parties and aspire towards the reunification of Ireland: personal and communal division is intertwined with political difference and creates a self-perpetuating or recurring cycle of antagonism. The underlying logic of the ethnic conflict approach is that conflicts such as the one in Northern Ireland are best understood by looking at people's political beliefs, communal allegiances, and constitutional aspirations. When these are perceived to be under threat, the logical response is to resist any loss of ground by closing off negotiations. Alternatively, when the opportunity arises to gain ground, the logical response is to try to better one's communal position.

Thus, the model is not only descriptive, but it is also predictive – the presence of antagonistic groups leads logically to conflict since, in zero-sum terms, for one side to win or to advance, the other has to lose or retreat. The model predicts downward spirals as communal leaders take up increasingly hard-line positions, making accommodation extremely difficult.

Ethnic conflict theorists have taken this logic one step further and attempted to explain how, despite a tendency for violence, conflict can be controlled. This entails setting out a political process and administrative institutions that separate the antagonistic factions, the idea being that in situations where political power cannot be negotiated, it needs to be divided. This idea, known as consociational theory, stands in direct contrast to both the Westminster first-past-the-post system, and the two-party system in America, which itself is saturated with ethnic politics. For example, unlike the American system of separating powers between the legislature, the judiciary, and the executive to achieve a balance, consociational theorists favour a much more rigid approach where vetoes or special rights and privileges (such as in education) are allocated to particular groups. In other words, rather than a Madisonian vision of 'ambition countering ambition' conflict is controlled by actually building political structures around ethnic groups, thereby effectively, institutionalising the underlying ethnic divisions.

Marxist explanations

The ethnic conflict model has challenged Marxist-inspired critiques, which stressed that the civil strife in the North was a product of discrimination and inequality of opportunity. Republicans, for example, borrowed from Marxist ideas and argued that Northern Ireland was a remnant of British imperialism: it suffered from the same disadvantages plaguing other colonial territories and its problems could only be resolved by British withdrawal. Although it was always difficult to fully justify this argument, given the extent of British economic support plus the material costs inflicted on British cities by the IRA bombing campaign inflicted, the idea of Britain being a colonial power echoed the traditional nationalist narrative of Irish history as being characterised by catastrophic events and a long struggle for freedom. At another level, the concentration on socio-economic factors inspired the attempts by both Labour and Conservative governments to bring the standard of living in Northern Ireland up to a par with that in the rest of the UK. However, as adherents of the ethnic conflict approach point out, the embedded communal allegiances and aspirations remain potent forces in Northern Ireland politics – a fact that is demonstrated at each election when ethno-nationalist parties campaign primarily on issues relating to their own communities.

The Marxist approach was substantively critiqued in the late 1970s and early 1980s by a group of historians working on the first major release of the papers of the Stormont governments, which, up until that time, had been closed for a fifty- rather than a thirty-year period. The most well-known example of this work was *The State in Northern Ireland* (first published in 1979) by Paul Bew, Peter Gibbon, and Henry Patterson. These authors focused particularly on class differences within the unionist community. They described how the rhetoric of unionist elites tapped into the fears of their grass-roots supporters regarding Irish nationalism and, in so doing, were able to maintain working-class support. As such, social and economic issues were rendered subservient to the need to protect the Union. The unionist leadership deployed huge propaganda resources at election times to persuade their supporters that the party was synonymous with the Union itself and that republicans and socialists were 'disloyal'. This 'siege mentality' is most visible during periods of constitutional or political uncertainty – the early 1920s and the early 1970s, for example, or, more recently, the Drumcree parading crisis (1996–7), which occurred at the beginning of the peace process.

While the siege mentality explanation continues to exert a major influence on how unionist politics are analysed; the reduction in the influence of Marxist insights has created certain gaps in areas other than 'high' politics. This is because the conflict was not just experienced through the lenses of nationalism and unionism. Working-class people in Northern Ireland suffered disproportionately in terms of deaths, injuries, and reduced life prospects. This was compounded by geography – certain working-class areas (north and west Belfast and the border regions in Fermanagh and South Armagh) bore the brunt of the conflict in comparison to the better-off areas of the North Down coast or the affluent Malone Road in Belfast.

According to the ethnic conflict model, alternative means of solidarity and identification – such as class, gender, age, or locale – do not exert the same pull as religion or nationality. A key problem with this perspective is how it silences and ignores the many ways in which the Troubles affected Northern Ireland. For example, gender and generational differences also affected both how people experienced the conflict and what they aspired towards at both personal and collective levels. In these instances, the tendency to reduce the Northern Ireland conflict to two antagonistic forces, while capturing something of the basic reality, creates many instances of voids and silences. Typically, the people who suffered during the conflict and whose stories were marginalised throughout the three decades of violence continue to be left out by the tendency to reduce the conflict to the basic common denominator of ethnicity.

The popularity of the ethnic conflict model to a certain extent ensures that those who benefited from the conflict continue to benefit from the peace while those who were left outside and forgotten continue to struggle for a political voice. Thus, the politicians, who espoused ideas about centuries-old conflict and everyone sharing responsibility for the past and the future, have, by and large, maintained their positions (and substantial remunerations) as the post-conflict political elite. Many ex-terrorists meanwhile have had their 'community standing' – which, in their eyes, was won through hardship and a willingness to get their hands dirty – recognised by various local initiatives such as the community restorative justice programmes. These programmes were originally established primarily as a means of ending punishment shootings of recalcitrant and anti-social youths and had the secondary purpose of filling the void of effective policing in many urban areas. Heavily subsidised by the British government, these programmes operate under the guiding ethos of republican (and to a lesser extent loyalist) distrust of the state and the understanding that the conflict was about valiant defence of vulnerable people rather than a series of sordid assassinations. Academics, community relations agencies, and peace and reconciliation gurus not only supervise and cheerlead for such programmes, they continue to perpetuate the idea that the past can be left behind in favour of a utopian future. In short, an entire 'peace process industry' reproduces dominant, ethnically based understandings of what the conflict was about and reproduces itself through the promise of blissful amnesia and a bright, shared future. Those people who dare to dissent from this post-conflict paradise, or who are inconsiderate enough to raise moral scruples, are roundly condemned as 'naive', or 'anti-Agreement', or silenced through the pragmatic threat that peace can only be maintained through moral compromise.[3]

Is Northern Ireland a religious conflict?

The tendency of some commentators and politicians to concentrate on a single feature of the conflict is replicated in the explanations given by some sociologists who emphasise the idea that religious difference was the central pivot on which contention turned. Thus religion is deeply implicated in the Troubles. We cannot hope to understand the durability of the historic divisions in Ireland if we fail to see that religious differences helped create those divisions in the first place and played an important role in sustaining them.[4]

In this view, the Northern Ireland conflict was not simply about ethnic identities; rather, those identities were expressed and given distinctive features through religious differences. For example, Claire Mitchell, an academic based at Queen's University, Belfast, has developed a forceful account of why religion is so important in Northern Irish politics.[5] Although the conflict was not over doctrinal or theological issues, Mitchell argues that the practices and rituals, and the various educative and parochial networks and groupings associated with the Catholic and Protestant churches, provided a means of socialisation or identification. In this way, even if people were not practising their religion on a regular basis, it still played an important role in who they saw themselves as being and, equally important, who they saw 'others' as being. Thus, people's daily experiences were refracted through a religious lens: religious identification helped people make sense of their interactions, it provided them with a basis in which to situate themselves in different contexts, and it allowed them to assess future prospects.

The major problem with this approach is that it fails to set out why religion should be a primary force in shaping the decisions that people make. Previous choices may in fact reduce our scope for action at later dates – once-available alternative courses of action may have been passed over and left behind. In other words, historical decisions may play a major role in setting out the types of choices available to people at different times, regardless of their political, social, or religious identification. Furthermore, the choices that we make at one point may actually influence the kinds of values we espouse later on – having placed all our eggs in one basket, so to speak, it is difficult to assess objectively the direction alternative decisions may have propelled us in. The case of the IRA campaign is illustrative of this dilemma – even though senior republicans knew early on that armed struggle was unlikely to achieve their war aim of reunification, it was seemingly impossible to repudiate violence without dishonouring those who had believed in it and had been imprisoned or killed for their beliefs. Values and allegiances do not just influence decision-making; decisions also create values and allegiances.

Indeed, when it comes to analysing what actually happened, religious sociologists tend to return to the historical narrative. Thus, it is impossible to explain Paisley's rise to prominence in the 1960s without reference to the disquiet caused by Terence O'Neill's reformist project and the civil rights movement. Despite Paisley's undoubted charismatic fundamentalism, it was the political context that provided him with a catalyst to attract supporters. That political context included the modernising project of Terence O'Neill and the growing calls for civil rights reforms. These factors, coupled with intensified British interest following the Labour victory of 1964, created a groundswell of unease among unionist grass roots and the Stormont elites. Fears for the constitutional future of Northern Ireland and suspicions that reform would be a slippery slope to a united Ireland helped to propel Paisley into the spotlight. The fracturing of the Unionist Party in the 1970s ensured that he would continue to be seen as a viable candidate for the leadership of unionism. His religious fundamentalism and political extremism in fact hindered his ascent. However, many unionists believed that Paisley's religious extremism and confrontational style of politics would alienate the population of the rest of the United Kingdom and, therefore, prove more threatening to the Union than the IRA's violence.

Was the conflict a result of irreconcilable ideologies?

Another variant on the tendency to highlight one factor above others is the idea that ideological differences drove the Northern Ireland conflict. The logic behind this notion is that if the Northern Ireland conflict was not simply caused by religious differences, was it therefore more to do with division at the level of ideas? Ideologies are ways of thinking about the world – they help us to interpret and make sense of the past and present and they provide us with visions to strive towards in the future. In this way they allow people to identify themselves with a wider group and can mobilise support towards achieving certain goals. By linking people with each other, ideologies also affect cultural perceptions and practices; they influence what politicians talk about and how current events are depicted in the wider media.

Often ideologies operate at an emotional rather than a strictly rational or intellectual level. Struggles to rectify perceived griev- ances or to equalise opportunities continue to be powerful means of motivating large numbers of people. When grievances and opportunities are tied to nationalist or ethnic sentiments, the result can be explosive. Ideologies are also open to change – in order to win or maintain support politicians continually emphasise different ideas and highlight certain arguments while downplaying others. Ideologies may challenge alternative viewpoints and values, but they may also be constantly revised and reworked by their own adherents as events transpire and the world around them changes.

This process of revision and contestation is often seen as a crucial factor in shaping Northern Ireland politics. Thus, so goes the story, nationalism and unionism are mutually exclusive; not only do nationalists identify with the Irish Republic and unionists with Britain, but, crucially, they aspire to radically different futures. The picture is further complicated by the internal politics of each ideological bloc. For example, within nationalism, Sinn

Féin has always argued that violent struggle is a necessary part of bringing about reunification, while the SDLP has claimed that unionists should be persuaded rather than coerced into a united Ireland. During periods of perceived threats to the constitutional status quo, unionism has experienced heightened unity – for example, during the Ulster Workers' Council Strike (1974) or the aftermath of the Anglo-Irish Agreement (1985). At other times it has been even more fractious than Northern nationalism – during the early 1970s, for example, William Craig advocated unilateral independence for Northern Ireland, Brian Faulkner argued for a return to devolved administration, while Ian Paisley advocated full integration within the UK system. Often these strategies reflect not only unionists' mistrust of nationalism, but also the suspicion unionists feel towards Westminster politicians.

As with the religious approach, simply concentrating on irreconcilable ideological differences may result in a skewed perspective. That political leaders may 'sell' ideological packages to different audiences might explain why local politicians appear much more militant and recalcitrant when speaking to their followers in Northern Ireland than they do when they are directing their words to international 'audiences' – the Irish or British governments or the White House. However, this does not account for why these audiences may buy into the messages in the first place. Although politicians may alter or revise their agendas, they often do so in a chaotic and piecemeal fashion. This is because the lessons we learn from the past are often fragmentary and based on idiosyncratic and limited viewpoints. Thus we rarely count the costs involved when decisions are successful – correspondingly, we may not reflect that a different decision may have led to the same or a better result. On the other hand, when choices result in failure, we tend to concentrate on the decisions that led to the undesirable outcome without considering whether other options would have also created the same result.

A further problem exists with the ideological approach insofar as it does not explain why it is that academics, political commentators, and elite politicians are able to discern subtle 'codes' or nuanced ideological shifts, while the grass roots blindly follow. That is to say, if politicians are working to scripts and rhetoric then why are academics able to take an objective viewpoint and deconstruct the meaning and intention behind the words in a manner that seems to escape ordinary voters? Indeed, the ideological approach may in fact overcomplicate matters – while, certainly, politicians tell their voters what they want to hear, this does not mean that the grass roots and the leaderships may actually share the same outlook and aspirations.

These problems lead to serious interpretive gaps when it comes to dealing with the history of the Northern Irish conflict. Thus, while it is true that Sinn Féin has placed a greater emphasis on human rights and equality issues, a broader perspective recognises that a reformist agenda was present within Irish nationalist discourse from the earliest days of the Troubles. Moreover, this stemmed from the lessons learned in the civil rights campaign that, by claiming political equality and the right to self-determination, one could, in turn, undermine partition. The argument that Sinn Féin adopted human rights rhetoric for strategic purposes – namely, to offset the fact that it would have to settle for less than a united Ireland – undoubtedly reflects something of the later reality. However, it not only neglects long-term trends within Northern nationalism, it also assumes too much. In other words, while the emphasising of equality rather than reunification allowed Sinn Féin to bolster its support during the 1990s and 2000s, there was no way that the party's leadership could have been certain that this particular strategy would be successful. The emphasis on short-term strategic shifts in rhetoric misses the central fact that it was the failure of the armed struggle and the obvious need for political alternative, rather than Machiavellian calculations, that transformed Sinn Féin's outlook and electoral success.

The Sinn Féin example serves to highlight a related problem with the ideological approach – that ideology did not drive the conflict at all; rather key decisions and omissions did. On the one hand, while ideology may influence the choices people make, it may also follow *from* those choices and be used in a self-justifying way after the fact. As pointed out in the previous chapter and by Alonso, for IRA volunteers political indoctrination nearly always followed recruitment. Although political calculation may have led a small percentage of volunteers to join, typically the recruitment process was to involve impressionable youths in serious violent acts soon after bringing them into the movement. Indoctrination into republican ideology only began at that point.

These children and young people were thus subjected to a deficient and tendentious 'political education' in which myth was increasingly confused with reality with the ultimate objective of legitimising IRA violence.[6]

Gendering the Northern Ireland conflict

Feminist scholars have been particularly scathing about the tendency of the dominant, ethnic conflict model to ignore gender politics and gender inequalities.[7] In a ground-breaking critique, Marysia Zalewski argues that gender is discussed by ethnic conflict theorists in such a way as to contain it or, more specifically, to treat it as something separate from the 'main' problem of ethnic division.[8] The lack of attention given by ethnic conflict theorists to gendered analyses of democracy, equality, identification, and violence should be unsurprising, given the tendency to incorporate all political dynamics under the rubric of antagonistic nationalisms.

In contrast, feminist scholars have demonstrated that the Northern Ireland conflict is intensely gendered. Both Irish nationalism and Ulster unionism propagate symbolic images of feminine purity and the importance of motherhood, and masculine valour and self-sacrifice – for example, no women were permitted to go on hunger strike in the early 1980s and instead the ideal of men sacrificing themselves for the good of the family and the nation was highlighted. Again, while both unionism and nationalism extol the value of motherhood, an integral part of the unionist identity is the idea that Protestant women should be dutiful wives and mothers and take a secondary role while their sons and husbands take responsibility for safeguarding the Union.[9]

These ideals shape communities by giving young nationalists and unionists values to aspire to. Furthermore, communal boundaries are reinforced by strict moral and sexual codes in which religious belief intertwines with politics to marginalise those individuals and groups who reject the prevailing mores – witness the emphatic denunciation of homosexuality by Iris Robinson (wife of the First Minister and DUP chair of the Assembly's Health Committee).[10]

The composition of the Northern Ireland Assembly illustrates the impact of gendered perspectives and the pitiful response of the local parties (see Table 2).

Table 2 Percentage of women represented in UK devolved assemblies, 1997–2007[11]

	Northern Ireland Assembly	Scottish Parliament	Welsh Assembly
1998	13%	N/A	N/A
1999	N/A	37%	40%
2003	16.7%	39.5%	50%
2007	16.7%	33%	47%

In response to the perceived opportunities created by the peace process, the Northern Ireland Women's Coalition (NIWC) formed in 1996 and attempted to promote a new way of 'doing' politics. Thus, while the party recognised that ethno-nationalist differences might mean that it would not reach a consensus on certain political and constitutional questions, nevertheless it would be able to encourage debate on socio-economic inequalities. The Coalition was instrumental in ensuring that the Good Friday Agreement included gender equality clauses and that a new position of Children's Commissioner would be established. However, following the polarisation of elite politics in the Assembly after 1998, the NIWC struggled to highlight the relevance of its cross-communal, pro-dialogue, and equality-based agenda. Having lost its two Assembly seats in 2003, the Coalition officially wound up in 2006.

Although the NIWC represented a radical departure in terms of the political culture of Northern Ireland, the danger the party faced was that gendered politics would be seen as something separate from mainstream (that is, in the Northern Ireland context, ethno-nationalist and constitutionalist) political concerns. As one community worker points out, ethno-national differences still form an important part of how people think of themselves:

> I'm a community relations worker. I'm a Protestant, I'm a Unionist, I'm a Loyalist. I didn't come here from Mars ... You know, I think because I'm a community relations worker I have to be something I'm not ... I am what I am and I make no apologies for it.[12]

The key dilemma for feminists is that the ethno-nationalist structure of Northern Ireland politics means that the pursuit of gender issues often flounders on communal politics – concerns over sexual equality or issues concerning sexual identity are refracted through political structures and political parties that are based on ethno-nationalist and religious difference.

History and the Northern Ireland conflict

Although Northern Ireland is a deeply divided society, it was historical decisions that created the specific conditions for conflict to thrive. In itself, ethno-nationalism does not lead to violence. In fact, ethnic groups are more likely to co-exist than enter into civil conflict.[13] Despite this, there is a tendency to equate the presence of ethno-nationalist division with conflict. In this view, the Northern Ireland conflict occurred due to the repeated failure to devise institutions that would accommodate the political divisions. In particular, it was only with the belated recognition by Britain that Dublin should be brought more fully on board that the framework for more peaceful politics began to emerge. As two scholars have pointed out:

> For the British government, the main change in the lead up to the peace process was simply the development of a more coherent political policy towards Northern Ireland. For much of the 1970s and 1980s, London primarily viewed Northern Ireland as a security problem. Political initiatives were not prioritised or were often pursued without inspiration.[14]

However, this type of analysis suffers from the same backwards-looking logic that republicans employ, for it implies that if only Britain had gained a greater understanding earlier, the years of violence could have been avoided.[15] A similar argument could be made for any of the groups (or states) involved. Not only does it smuggle in certain elitist assumptions – 'if only "they" had been as smart as "us" then the conflict would have been shortened' – it also sharply contradicts the historical evidence. Britain *did* try to involve Dublin, power-sharing institutions *were* set up in the 1970s, but the result was only to destabilise the situation. Indeed, an argument can be made that the Anglo-Irish Agreement delayed the establishment of power sharing: the

SDLP were effectively prepared to settle for Dublin involve-ment, while Ulster unionism was left directionless. Britain did not fail to learn the 'correct' lessons nor did it only learn the 'wrong' ones; indeed, as the state papers reveal, government officials were only too well aware of the limitations on what they could purposefully achieve. The ambiguity and apparent contradictions in British policymaking occurred as a result of these limitations, not because of a lack of vision.

The circular reasoning of the advocates of the ethnic conflict model in particular lends itself to misleading interpretations of the Northern Ireland conflict. Starting from assumptions about the antagonistic nature of ethno-nationalism, scholars argue that the warring factions need to be inculcated – through political or economic incentives or through imposing a settlement – into the 'correct' way of conducting themselves. Without such checks, so the argument goes, ethno-nationalist sentiment and violence will spiral out of control. Thus, as one political scientist has put it:

> While Northern Ireland lacked the external pillars of strong Anglo-Irish relations, internal intra-elite stability, based on an acceptance of Northern Ireland's new political situation, was also missing.[16]

Beneath the opaque language lies a patronising platitude: had London and Dublin enforced their will on the local populace earlier, much of the Troubles would not have happened.[17]

There are three steps that lead to these conclusions. First, the assumption that the conflict was to do with ethno-nationalist antagonism becomes a self-fulfilling prophecy: the historical record is cherry-picked to reveal signs that if only the govern-ments had learned quicker, then the 'natives' could have been controlled. Second, after-the-fact justifications from surviving witnesses are sought but rarely subjected to any form of critical analysis – the 'mistakes' and the 'correct decisions' are recycled without asking whether alternatives would have turned out differently. The final step is to ignore the archival material and instead to tout supposed lessons from Northern Ireland in other troubled areas such as the Middle East, South-East Asia, or the Balkans as a transferable, all-purpose peace process model.

The assumption that the Northern Ireland conflict was fought primarily over incompatible conceptions of belonging and belief has generated heated debates over how the conflict might be resolved. Briefly stated, these debates centre around whether the divide could be broken down through cross-communal engagement and the promotion of integrated education, or whether it is best to begin with the divide and ensure the protection of rights for each community. The first position favours the development of grass-roots cooperation and the nurturing of 'civic society' ideas based on shared responsibilities. The end goal, in this instance, is the transformation or integration of polarised and entrenched identities into a more open and accommodative political culture.[18]

This approach contrasts sharply with the ethnic conflict school, which tends to begin with the assumption that ethnonational identities are quite durable and resistant to change. Instead of responsibilities, the focus in this instance is on group rights and the segregation of the communal blocs. This is achieved by working at the level of 'high politics' – institutional design and the separation of political power among the local elites.[19] Traditionally, government policy has been a mixture of the two approaches: while attempting to foster dialogue between the local parties, the British government has also encouraged integrated education and civic society initiatives.

An emerging consensus

While it may be true that the questions we ask about the past are always influenced by our present concerns, it is also the case that the past is not entirely changeable. As such, it is perhaps unsurprising that the Northern Ireland conflict has not only proven to be problematic for historians, but that, as a result of contentious debates and the increasing availability of primary source material, certain broad areas of consensus are beginning to emerge. For example, the papers relating to the Stormont government, the Unionist Party, and the Orange Order reveal that it is no longer credible to speak of a 'Unionist monolith'. It is undeniable that the Unionist Party held sole control of the Northern Ireland state from the 1920s until 1972. However, that control was always too uncertain and too nuanced to be total or 'hegemonic'. The sudden collapse of the Northern Ireland state between 1968 and 1972 in and of itself demonstrated the instability at the centre of unionist politics. It is also undeniable that discrimination did exist and that Catholics were proportionately worse off than Protestants under the Stormont system. However, discrimination was not wholesale but concentrated in specific locales and in certain aspects of local government employment and administration. Insofar as the local government franchise was linked to home and business ownership, many Catholic and Protestant workers were left without a vote at that level.

When modernisation was attempted in the 1960s, Terence O'Neill's economic reforms proved wholly inadequate for tackling the political divisions that marred Northern Irish society. O'Neill's ideas about using the market to improve individuals' standards of living had little meaning for the working class of either community. In part, this led O'Neill to underestimate the depth of ethnic identification and he singularly failed to recognise that rising standards of living could not transform nationalists into unionists. O'Neill's premiership did, however, provide a catalyst for the Northern Ireland civil rights movement, which set out to confront discriminatory practices – and, while it was never a communist conspiracy and was too broad based to be simply a republican front, it is also true that its adherents displayed a remarkable naivety in importing the 'US model' of marching and mass rallies. Although these tactics were successful in provoking the police, they also broke communal taboos surrounding the importance of geography and security and thus served to raise tensions, suspicions, and fears. The reluctance of the British state to take decisive political action to accompany the deployment of troops in 1969 also contributed to a downward spiral in inter-communal relations. British decision-makers frequently sent out contradictory signals that did little to alleviate the situation – thus, heavy-handed military tactics such as the introduction of internment (1971) took place against the backdrop of regular talks with the IRA. Again, despite the polarisation of the two communities and the wider context of political uncertainty, it was the decision by Belfast republicans to take the war to the British troops in 1970 that opened the door to a broader and bloodier conflict than had hitherto been the case.

The Northern Ireland conflict emerged and persisted due to historical choices. These choices were influenced by ideological or political preferences, coloured by perceived grievances and opportunities, and shaped by previous events and received 'truths' about history – nevertheless, at each step alternatives existed. During the period between the early 1920s and late 1960s, Ulster unionism could have been more accommodating to the nationalist minority; likewise, nationalist political leaders could have been more understanding of unionists' aspirations and fears. The civil rights campaign could have refrained from marching through Protestant areas during the late 1960s. The IRA could have decided that an armed campaign against British forces and the Protestant community was never likely to convince unionists to join a united Ireland. Even when it became clear that the military campaign was highly unlikely to 'drive the Brits into the sea', the IRA could have decided that it was pointless and (even by its own standards) morally suspect to send its members out to kill and be killed.

Even after the imposition of direct rule, the political representatives of unionism and nationalism did little to encourage accommodation or understanding. Again, although they reflected deeper ideological divisions to some extent, it was the choices and omissions by the local representatives that contributed to the entrenched divisions of Northern Irish political life during the 1970s. While dialogue and compromise would have proven to be difficult amidst the escalating violence, little imagination or understanding was shown by either the SDLP or the unionist parties. Despite calls for power sharing and an 'agreed Ireland', the SDLP did little to persuade unionists that their best interests lay in ending partition. Instead, they banked political gains – such as the ending of Stormont and the Anglo-Irish Agreement – in order to move further towards greater Dublin involvement in the running of the North. Both the Ulster Unionist Party and the DUP also pursued insular, inward-looking politics. Both groupings resisted power sharing and the Irish dimension, without offering any credible alternative – save for Brian Faulkner's discredited 1971 proposal for majority rule with committee seats for the SDLP.

While New Labour politicians and conflict transformation academics may court the paramilitaries, it is important to note that, despite social deprivation and multiple instances of atrocities being inflicted by state forces, the majority of working-class people did not join paramilitary groupings. Although ex-political prisoners play crucial roles helping to diffuse tension in urban working-class areas, their 'standing' in those areas was won and maintained through violence. While these community leaders claim that they only did what others wanted but were afraid to do themselves, such self-justifications should not be allowed to obscure the fact that the overwhelming majority of people in Northern Ireland – both middle and working class – refused to join paramilitary groups but nevertheless continued to suffer from the consequences of the paramilitaries' war.

The tendency to resort to ethno-nationalism to explain the conflict is common among scholars, political commentators, and politicians themselves. This chapter has pointed out that while ethno-national difference may describe the main feature of the conflict, in itself it does not actually explain why the conflict began, why it persisted, or why it drew to an uncertain close. By ignoring the importance of specific choices and omissions, the ethno-nationalist approach tends to gloss over historical nuance and completely ignores questions to do with culpability or responsibility – that is, who did what and why. In so doing, ethno-nationalism tends to recycle the dominant myths and narratives surrounding the conflict – in particular, the idea that it was over primordial antagonisms, which can be overcome through the manufacturing of an elite agreement. The result is to allocate responsibility for the conflict to everyone and no-one, and thereby create a confusing and sinister complicity between those who suffered the most from the conflict and those who remained in powerful positions.

Conclusion: Troubled legacies

The politics of change

When the mainstream paramilitary groups called their ceasefires in 1994 Belfast had sixteen interface walls. Known locally by the euphemistic name 'peace walls', their purpose was to separate one community from the other. They run along roads, and encircle housing estates and primary schools. Since the ceasefire, most of these have been extended or heightened. A further nine have been built, bringing the total of such walls across the North to forty-six. These figures do not include the underground wall that separates the Catholic and Protestant dead in Belfast City Cemetery.[1]

The growth in peace walls in Belfast has occurred due to a gradual worsening of inter-communal relations in the decade and a half since the 1994 ceasefire. Despite the ending of the paramilitaries' campaigns in the 1990s, statistics in virtually every area bear witness to the growing sectarianisation of Northern Irish society. First, violence has continued within and between the two communities, taking the form of attacks on symbolically important properties (church halls, Gaelic Athletic Association (GAA) clubs, Orange Lodges) or rioting.[2]

The growth in sectarianism may be attributable in part to the residual polarising effects of the conflict. Again, as was pointed out above in relation to party policymaking in the DUP and Sinn Féin, while the balkanised institutions at Stormont serve to reflect communal division, they also serve to perpetuate it in very real terms. Another element which cannot be ignored, however, is the continued presence and operation of paramilitary groups. For instance, between 1994 and 2004 there were 1129 punishment attacks across Northern Ireland, which constituted between 0.2% (1995) and 16.4% (2001) of the total number of assaults in the North. The continued activity of organised paramilitary factions is also evident in the numbers of politically motivated deaths in the province. Thus, between 1983 and 1993, 857 people were killed by paramilitaries; the effect of the ceasefires was simply to reduce that figure to 225 people killed between 1994 and 2005. Again, bombings and shootings continued even after the ceasefires. For example, there were 5204 shootings and 3660 bombings in the decade prior to the ceasefires (1983–93), which fell to 2505 shootings and 1660 bombings in the subsequent decade of the 'peace process' (1994–2004).[3]

Contrary to the arguments advanced by those who believed that the best way of proceeding was to divide up political power and portion it out to the leaders of the communal blocs, the institutions established under the Belfast Agreement have failed to tackle the escalating sectarianism and division that characterises everyday life across the North. Furthermore, the 'power-sharing' institutions have perpetuated division at the elite level by offering political parties incentives to radicalise rather than moderate their policies. Both Sinn Féin and the DUP have eclipsed the more centrist SDLP and UUP as the main representatives of nationalism and unionism, and strengthened their position at Stormont. Arguably, it is not presently in the interests of either party to withdraw from the Northern Ireland Assembly; neither is it in their interests to pursue accommodative politics.

This has been evident from the earliest days of the devolved institutions. For example, soon after taking office, the then Sinn Féin Minister of Health, Bairbre de Brún decided to close the

Jubilee Maternity Hospital in a predominantly Protestant area of Belfast, leaving the Royal Victoria Hospital in the Catholic area of west Belfast as the principal site of maternity services in the city. Although de Brún argued that the decision was made on the basis of sound planning, her handling of the issue seemed questionable as the Assembly's Health Committee had advised against the move.[4] Although some political commentators predicted the emergence of a moderate political culture,[5] in fact neither the DUP nor Sinn Féin have revised their long-term goals in any shape or form. Thus, in February 2008, Sinn Féin began consultations on a 'roadmap for unity', while Peter Robinson announced the following month that majoritarian 'voluntary coalition' remained the DUP's 'preferred' option.[6]

What, then, can we say about the changes that have taken place in Northern Ireland's recent past? The new political structures in Northern Ireland have created incentives for the local elites to pursue their long-term goals through political channels. However, they have singularly failed to tackle entrenched sectarian attitudes and have perpetuated a political culture based on division and confrontation rather than moderation and accommodation. One change has been that, while politics continues to operate along adversarial lines, the Northern Ireland Assembly has laid the foundations for a system of government based on localised grievances and ethnic one-up-man-ship. The new institutional structures have brought Sinn Féin into government and made it extremely difficult for the IRA even to contemplate returning to violence. Yet, as the statistics reveal, deep-seated animosities pervade Northern Irish society and elite division simply mirrors ground-level contention. On the streets of Belfast, these animosities continue to be played out in various ethnic confrontations. A key part of political life in the city includes continued conflict over housing allocation and the intimidation of families who find themselves in the 'wrong' estates; annual parades disputes; and a culture of almost ritualised rioting. Across the North, territory, demography, and commemoration remain crucial indicators of communal strength, and the overwhelming trend is for localities to become more segregated rather than less.[7]

Peace has come to Northern Ireland but, as the Assembly's politics demonstrate, it is one based on an uneasy acceptance of the importance of the constitutional and communal divide. The quiescence is itself largely based on people's experiences of the conflict – not only do the decisions made in the past continue to affect political dynamics in the present, but also people's expectations of what form politics should take is largely determined by their perceptions of what has gone before. That the North's political culture is one of détente and confrontation is, thus, hardly surprising: the collective experience of moderation or accommodation is overwhelmingly negative – the single previous experiment in power-sharing democracy lasted a mere five months in 1974. Therefore, not only has the past shaped and constrained politics in the present, but the enduring legacy of contention and confrontation also continues to influence people's views about the past. This two-way relationship – experiences of the past influence perceptions in the present; though perceptions in the present also reinforce views about the past – has ensured that the very history of the Troubles has become another site of confrontation.

This history is based on selective remembering and the careful massaging of favoured stories. Both republicans and loyalists give special value to commemorative practices and symbolic sites. Memorials to fallen terrorists (primarily murals and memorials) and the rituals of commemoration attached to them have a dual function: they signify territorial control of certain areas and act as reminders of who the dominant voices are. In other words, paramilitary memorials are concerned with the past insofar as specific ideas about the past can be used to further political ends in the present – they remind local people about the sacrifices paramilitaries made for them and emphasise the idea that paramilitaries' actions (which, of course, are not referred to specifically or in any detail) were carried out in order to defend their people. Thus only thirty per cent of 2074 civilian deaths are commemorated in the public sphere, compared with almost every one of the 1574 combatants. Again, the fact that such memorials and rituals are intensely gendered is no accident: men lead the unveiling ceremonies while women watch; and, on the murals and memorial statues, men are represented as valiant warriors while women are passive 'victims'.[8]

In a similar fashion, attitudes to the past informed the complex negotiations leading up to the Belfast Agreement. The persistence of long-term political aims has effectively meant that the inter-communal struggle has moved to another, less violent, level. Since the fundamental goals of the local political parties remain largely untouched, their historical *raisons d'être* continue to underpin their modern agendas. Understandably, the past continues to play a major role in driving forward party politics under the new institutions. This situation has been compounded due to the fact that the ending of the 'overt' war in the 1990s was also a messy process that left all sides – republicans, loyalists, and the British Army – able to claim victories and forced none to confront their pasts. The past was therefore not 'left out' of the peace process in case it would cause it to unravel – the past continued (and continues) to determine the shape taken by, and the pace of, the North's political progress.

Dealing with the past

The question of how to deal with the legacies of the conflict has become the principal battleground in the political struggles in the North. Since the late 1990s, various institutions have been established to try to tackle those legacies. However, these bodies have been subject to the same historically conditioned constraints that shaped the conflict. In other words, it is simplistic to assume that Northern Ireland is moving from a 'bad' past to a 'good' future when the divisions that drove the violence continue to define contemporary politics.[9]

The first such institution was the Victims' Commission, established in October 1997. The Commission was headed by the former head of the Northern Ireland Civil Service Sir Kenneth Bloomfield and was arguably a direct response to the inclusion of Sinn Féin in political talks, by affording prominence to the concerns and grievances of unionists and members of the security forces.[10] Bloomfield's report recommended a series of measures for dealing with victims' concerns, including giving greater compensation to victims and victims' support groups; the creation of an official ombudsman to deal with victims' demands; a fund to assist children whose parents were killed; giving greater priority to the treatment of trauma and pain; and improved employment opportunities for victims. The report also recommended the institution of a memorial day for victims and the setting up of an archive for victims' stories. While it stopped short of calling for an official truth and reconciliation commission, it suggested that such a mechanism may be appropriate in the future.[11] Bloomfield's report came under heavy criticism from nationalist groups, who felt that it ignored victims of state-sponsored violence – containing only two paragraphs on this issue in its seventy pages. This sense of nationalist disillusion was further compounded when the British government appointed the then Security Minister, Adam Ingram, as Minister for Victims in May 1998. The following month, Ingram established the Victims Liaison Unit within the Northern Ireland Office to implement Bloomfield's core recommendations concerning financial assistance.

The January 1998 establishment of an inquiry into 'Bloody Sunday' alleviated nationalists' anxieties to a certain extent. The inquiry, which was chaired by Lord Saville, commenced in March 2000 and examined the actions of both state and non-state actors on the day in question. Although the inquiry has yet to publish its findings, its effect on Northern Irish and British politics has been profound. The fact that over half of its reported £181 million costs have been spent on lawyers' fees has not only contrasted with the working-class status of many of the victims' families, but has also led to questions over whether the money could have been better spent elsewhere. Again, the adversarial, courtroom operation of the inquiry has meant that finding new evidence is a long process, leading many to question its value. Finally, the open-ended remit and terms of investigation of the inquiry have influenced the Labour government's decision to severely curtail the subsequent Butler and Hutton inquiries into the Iraq War.

The 1998 Belfast Agreement did not provide for any specific mechanisms for dealing with the past. Regardless of any unspoken consensus on deciding not to deal with the past, the negotiating process and the final Agreement were saturated with the legacy of the conflict: the past was an intrinsic part of the politics of the Agreement. These politics included a passing reference to the need to acknowledge the 'suffering of the victims of violence as a necessary element of reconciliation'. Victims' issues warranted three paragraphs on the eighteenth page of the thirty-page document. The Agreement also provided for the 'accelerated release of prisoners' and set out a two-year time frame for this to occur. Although only prisoners affiliated to organisations that the Secretary of State judged to be on ceasefire could benefit from the scheme, there was no specific linking of the releases to arms decommissioning. The Agreement also called on the British and Irish governments to 'provide support both prior to and after release' to help the prisoners reintegrate into society. While the release of prisoners was integral to bringing and keeping Sinn Féin and the IRA on board, the gulf between the treatment of perpetrators and victims angered many people in Northern Ireland. For unionists in particular, the failure to link prisoner releases to decommissioning compounded this problem. While the IRA refused to hand over arms, since republicans claimed it remained undefeated, unionists believed that the Agreement had failed to provide similar benefits for them. The sense of outrage over prisoner releases and decommissioning contributed enormously to the subsequent growth of unionist disillusionment with the Agreement.

As was mentioned in chapter 4, the Agreement also called for a review of policing in Northern Ireland, to deal with nationalists' historic alienation from the police. These measures had several specific knock-on effects regarding the role that the legacy of the conflict plays in contemporary events. For example, the Ombudsman's 2007 report into collusion between the RUC's Special Branch and loyalist paramilitaries highlighted abuses in specific police operations. The main UVF informant at the centre of the case, Mark Haddock, was accused in the Dáil of carrying out at least twenty-one murders, including not only Catholics but also fellow loyalists and a Protestant clergyman. A further development in police reform was the decision to set up a PSNI Historical Enquiries Team in 2005 to investigate 3269 unsolved murders in Northern Ireland. The team, which currently comprises 175 staff from Northern Ireland, the Republic, and Britain, has come under intense political scrutiny. For example, in 2007, the then Secretary of State, Peter Hain, pointed out that:

> Huge amounts of money are involved which cannot be spent on meeting the concerns of today. Recent political progress in Northern Ireland should make us pause and ask whether re-living or even re-fighting the Troubles in the courtroom or the public inquiry or through police investigation is really a healthy way forward.[12]

In response to that recent progress – namely, the restoration of a devolved administration in May 2007 – Hain established a Consultative Group on the Past. Co-chaired by Lord Robin Eames, the former Church of Ireland Primate of Ireland, and Dennis Bradley, a former Catholic priest, the Group was tasked with 'finding the best way to deal with the legacy of the past' and making 'recommendations on ways to support Northern Ireland society in building a shared future'.

The Group launched its Report[13] amid chaotic scenes in the Europa Hotel, Belfast, on 28 January 2009, during which the Chief Constable Hugh Orde and Sinn Féin President Gerry Adams looked on passively as victims' relatives jostled and argued with one another. Much of the anger was sparked by the proposal to offer £12,000 to the families of both innocent victims and those of terrorists. While the rejection of any 'hierarchy of victims' by the Group reflected the policy already in place in the Republic, the public outcry effectively meant that the other proposals were overlooked by the media. The Group argued that a Legacy Commission could deal with unresolved issues arising from the Troubles. This Commission, the Group said, would negate the need for any further public inquiries, while its suggested five-year term of office would presumably allow the British government to draw a line under its official responsibilities for the conflict.

The main criticism of these proposals relates to how they deal with the *present*. Quite how sectarianism and social division can be managed when it is institutionalised in the communal carve-up of political power at the elite level of Stormont is carefully avoided. Furthermore, while the Legacy Commission will have the power to compel the release of suppressed govern-mental inquiries into shoot-to-kill and collusion policies (the Stalker and the Stevens Reports), there is no indication that the Group gave much thought as to how the Commission is to acquire documents or submissions from the paramilitaries. The

Group has suggested that 'moral' pressure will create compliance; however, if the republican and loyalist communities could not prevent almost 4000 deaths, there is little to suggest that they will be able to convince terrorists to place themselves before a judicial process.

It is difficult to sustain an argument that the Consultative Group were simply politically naive. In fact, as with the other facets of the peace process industry, everything about their approach to the past is intensely value-laden – specific lessons are cherry-picked from the past and awkward facts are ignored. A key theme of this industry is that 'We must turn to the future and break the cycle of hatred'[14] – or, as the epigraph of the Report puts it: 'To look backward for a while is to refresh the eye, to restore it, and to render it more fit for its prime function of looking forward.' In other words, the vast majority of people who did not join terrorist organisations must be reconciled to the murderous actions of others. If the Group's proposals go ahead, Northern Ireland's 'shared future' – for the next five years, at least – will consist of being forced to listen to the self-serving, post hoc justifications that have already served as the basis for countless terrorist speeches, autobiographies, and other writings.[15]

The Consultative Group's remit overlaps with the decision of the First and Deputy First Ministers of the Assembly to appoint four commissioners to the newly established Commission for Victims and Survivors. Certainly, the four reflected the religious divide (two Protestants, two Catholics) and political sensibilities (Mike Nesbitt, a former newsreader; Bertha McDougal, the widow of an RUC reservist killed by republicans; Patricia McBride, whose brother was killed by the SAS and father by loyalists; and Brendan McAllister of the NGO, Mediation Northern Ireland). However, Ian Paisley and Martin McGuinness denied that there were behind-the-scenes disagreements concerning the appointments and instead claimed that, despite only one post being advertised, four commissioners would 'be better equipped to deal with the needs of victims and survivors'.[16] The Commission began holding public consultations in the summer of 2008, but, at the time of writing, they have yet to issue a report.

The politics of victimhood and the victims of politics

Beyond platitudes and self-absolutions, the divergent experiences of the Troubles give rise to a range of explanatory narratives. Arguably, the diverse experiences of violence, suspicion, and sectarianism militate against the emergence of any single explanation or 'truth' about the conflict that could gain widespread acceptance. Just as different stories about history and different modes of belonging inspired the choices that drove the conflict, so too do these different experiences and competing versions of the past pervade the present. In this way, contemporary politics in Northern Ireland are not simply about antagonistic explanations. Neither does the answer to the divergent experiences lie in simply recollecting the past in greater detail. Rather, contemporary politics is about both competing histories and competing ways of forgetting.

Nowhere is this more evident than in the cult of victimhood that has arisen naturally out of people's different ways of interpreting the past and explaining the actions and beliefs of their own community. Marie Breen Smyth has pointed out that a politics of victimhood first developed in Northern Ireland owing to the perception that attacks on communities or families mainly came from 'outsiders'.[17] Violent attacks not only create common grievances, they also justify retaliation: victims are, by definition, vulnerable and in need of assistance to help to restore the balance of power and protect them from further attacks. Whereas loyalist paramilitaries justified their actions on the basis of providing defence on behalf of their communities from attacks against the IRA; republican paramilitaries claimed that they were simply protecting their communities from 'British imperialism' and 'loyalist death squads'. The immediate result was an entrenched perception of victimhood and the escalation and recycling of violence.

The politics of victimhood has also removed the need for admission of responsibility for violent actions – specifically, individual responsibility. Loyalists, for instance, have pointed out that in a time of peace it is now impossible to understand the context that drove them to seek to protect their own communities during the conflict:

> Revisiting what was done in the past ... runs the risk of not being understood by the current/younger generation. Children today will probably find it difficult to imagine the threats and fears that inspired their fathers to take up arms.[18]

The appeal to history – the idea that 'if you had been there, you would have done the same' – should not be allowed to provide a cloak to provide cover for previous actions. Although history is about interpretation, it is also about facts and certain facts do not change. Indeed, the idea that murderers are victims too ought to be summarily dismissed. As the historian Richard Evans has remarked in another context: 'A murderer is a murderer, however persuasive the mitigating circumstances of the fact.'[19] Despite the prevalence of communal fears and ethnic prejudices the Northern Irish conflict was about choices made or avoided. Although the paramilitaries recruited impressionable young people, the business of sectarian killing involved a series of choices. Certainly, the paramilitary leaderships – the loyalists involved in the first killings in 1966 and the republicans involved in deciding to take the war to the 'Brits' in 1969 – bear a greater responsibility than most, but the casual indifference to individuals on the 'other side' was not a natural, excusable character trait. Each community was 'provoked' by acts of violence, but only a tiny minority of the North's population became involved in the paramilitary campaigns.

To date, the loyalist position on dealing with the past is perhaps the most detailed of any of the local political groups. While they point out that 'unless our stories are told, the future teaching of history will remain one-sided', loyalists are reluctant to support a truth recovery process at present. Among their concerns is the idea that 'many wounds are still too raw'. In other words, societal hurts are still too close to the surface and in revisiting the past, old animosities may be stoked up. Furthermore, loyalists fear that in any such process the odds would be stacked against their version(s) of history. Thus they feel that not only are republicans adept at 'spinning' stories, but also that neither they nor the British state would honestly engage with such a process. Again, loyalists perceive an overt hostility from what they call 'middle unionism' as well as a latent bitterness towards paramilitaries from their traditional Protestant working-class support-base. As regards the latter, loyalists believe that by raking over events in the past, ex-prisoners and community workers would face renewed alienation from the communities they are now living and working in. Taken one step further, they argue, any revisiting of the past could put the lives of former paramilitaries and their families in danger. On a pragmatic basis, loyalists also point out that, in the absence of any form of amnesty, it would not make sense for activists to implicate themselves in crimes.

Contemporary political calculations also inform republicans' approach to the past and attitudes to the idea of a truth recovery process. By its own account, Sinn Féin is more open to the idea of truth recovery than loyalists. Thus it claims that: 'it is clear that the issue of "truth" needs to be addressed'.[20] Sinn Féin's preferred model for dealing with the past is through an independent and international commission. It argues that any process should be politically neutral and victim-centred, and should have full cooperation and disclosure from all relevant parties. The priority is, therefore, a holistic approach that encompasses not just the 'combatant groups' but also the media, civic society, the judiciary, and state institutions. The objectives of such a process, for republicans, are 'to learn the lessons of the past so that mistakes will not be repeated' and 'to enable society to build the peace'.

The British government has been reticent about initiating such a process. Although the government's inquiry into the issue of dealing with the past was curtailed by the 2005 general election, its interim report set out several findings that indicate the current position.[21] For instance, the government points out that the very lack of consensus about the past in general and about truth recovery in particular, makes it very difficult to envisage a formal process at present. According to the report, several factors militate against such a process: the potential of large sections of the community opting out; the widespread resistance to the idea of an 'official' version of history; a lack of conviction that violence is at an end; and the possibility of exacerbating political tensions. The fact that the British state was not simply an innocent bystander or arbitrator but was involved in perpetuating the conflict, militarily and politically, has led some commentators to reach similar conclusions to republicans and loyalists. Thus commentators have voiced suspicions that state cooperation – and that of the army in particular – would not be straightforward.[22]

Political contingencies therefore affect the British approach to the legacy of the conflict in two ways: first, policy implementation is severely constrained by divisions on the ground. Second, indefinite delay of a formal process favours certain elements within the state security apparatus. Despite an official willingness to embrace 'truth', similar self-serving and self-regarding calculations are also discernible in republicans' attitudes to the past. As the journalist Fintan O'Toole pointed out, republicans have all but internalised a 'double-standard' approach to the past. Thus, the Sinn Féin MP Conor Murphy can call for an independent inquiry into the killing of Eddie Fullerton, a party councillor, in 1991, but the IRA is reluctant to adopt the same openness to its own actions. O'Toole refers specifically to the killings of Bernard Teggart, a fifteen-year-old boy with a mental age of eight, in Belfast and Kathleen Feeney, a fourteen-year-old girl in Derry in 1973. The IRA issued apologies in 2004 and 2005 respectively. But, says O'Toole, 'If the IRA could establish 32 years later that one of their own members [rather than the British Army] killed Kathleen Feeney, it is almost inconceivable that Martin McGuinness [the then Derry OC] did not know this at the time.' O'Toole points out that the IRA covered up both murders – which it knew about all along – for over three decades before issuing 'laconic, anonymous statements following secretive investigations', while its political representatives demand 'nothing short of full accountability' from the British state.[23]

Loyalists, too, are guilty of double standards. For example, their recent statement on the past alluded to the collective responsibility of Catholics ('the nationalist community') for 'their armed groups' and claimed that this alleged responsibility provided the rationale for their own armed campaign. This explanation of the Troubles, the document says, 'is something that neither the state nor middle unionism will accept (at least not openly)'. However, contrary to loyalist perceptions, the reason that neither unionists nor the British state accept the argument is understandable. Indeed, loyalists apply the same logic to themselves in the document – namely, that it is individuals who bear the brunt of violence; and individuals cannot justly be held to account for the actions of others. As with republicans, the loyalist argument that different standards apply in peacetime is not a sufficient basis for dealing (or not dealing) with the past: the attempted explanation of murder simply covers over what happened and requires victims to 'move on' with their perpetrators.

It is certainly understandable for paramilitaries to claim that they want the conflict 'to remain buried in the past ... [and] want to draw a line under those times'.[24] However, as the German philosopher Theodor Adorno pointed out, in reality this attitude underpins the not inconsiderable accomplishment of rendering null and void the responsibility of the perpetrators for their actions and removing victims' sole power – remembrance. Adorno argued against the temptation to explain away murder and the idea that 'everything should be forgotten and forgiven'. He emphasised that this approach to a violent past is most often 'practiced by those party supporters who committed the injustice'. Furthermore, he said, it reverses the moral distinction between victims and perpetrators: 'in the house of the hangman one should not speak of the noose, otherwise one might seem to harbour resentment'.[25]

The reluctance of the British state or the paramilitary groups to publicly acknowledge their past actions and seek forgiveness, however, does not mean that victims' concerns are doomed to being marginalised. Indeed, the proliferation of victims' groups and the perception that the conflict has ended has brought issues concerning the past more and more into public discourse. Yet it is unrealistic to expect victims' groups or civil society initiatives to foster new narratives about the past. As the history of the conflict reveals, politics at the grass roots are often as sectarian as those of any politician. Again, the historical narratives of civic society factions may be as biased as those held by political elites.

The politics of the Agreement

Dealing with the past encompasses victims' needs but also takes in wider concerns to do with how we remember and how we interpret the conflict. There is no reason to expect a truth recovery process to create a new political climate. Indeed, the very lack of accountability and scrutiny under the present political system does not bode well for anyone desiring accountability for the past. While the politics of the past shaped the current power-sharing structures, those same structures ensure the continued dominance of received narratives concerning the past: narratives based on self-righteous struggle and dignified victimhood. Certainly, not everyone in Northern Ireland is a victim; however, everyone is responsible for the past. The problem is that the institutional legacy of the past – the communal carve-up of power that constitutes devolved government – effectively works against any 'working through' history of the conflict.

The main effect of the Northern Ireland Assembly and the Good Friday Agreement has been to bring to an end the war between and among the paramilitaries and the British state. However, it is a mistake to draw the lesson that the particular institutional set-up was responsible for the ending of the violence – other, less inflexible structures might have brought about the same result. Indeed, administratively, the powers of the Northern Ireland Assembly are extremely limited:

> They [the MLAs] don't have any tax-raising powers. They didn't ask for them. They don't have power to alter health and social service provisions. They didn't ask. All they can do is tinker with the money Britain provides.[26]

The primary power that the Assembly does exercise, however, is over the continued functioning of divisive beliefs. First, the statistical evidence reveals that it has been unable to tackle embedded sectarianism – other than to exacerbate communal division. Second, the power-sharing structures have frozen in place certain narratives about the Troubles. These narratives are based around the parties' interpretations of the conflict and form the basis of their policy agendas and underlying rationale. Thus, the Northern Irish past remains divided in contemporary perceptions because the objective conditions that engendered division continue to exist. Insofar as our identities are bound up with narratives about history, the Assembly cements societal division.

The problem for the Assembly and the politicians it 'empowers' is that identities are flexible. What we remember about the past is intimately associated with when we remember – in other words, the past shapes our present identities, but our present circumstances also affect how we view the past. This means that no interpretation about the conflict is ever set in stone. As the previous chapter pointed out, historical evidence has dethroned accepted academic ideas concerning the importance of fixed ethno-national identities: it is impossible, credibly, to ignore the fact that the conflict was about choices and perceptions and to maintain that it was simply about antagonistic beliefs. In a similar way, people's experiences and memories of the conflict are fluid and will change. Although the constitutional question may well remain, the continued questioning of the types of historical explanations offered by the Assembly's politicians may create problems of legitimacy. This is because the Good Friday Agreement's institutions were created on a certain model of interpretation that assumed the conflict was about fixed and antagonistic identities and the continued dominance of received historical explanations. That this model does not reflect the small portion of the population that favour cross-communal accommodation is almost beside the point. The real potential for a crisis of legitimacy arises as the vast majority of the population continue to take responsibility for their past. Insofar as the Assembly can forestall or circumvent that process of questioning, its existence will be guaranteed. However, in the long run, the politics of the Agreement will surely have to come to terms with the politics of the past.

March 2009: the return of tragedy

Tragedy returned to the streets of Northern Ireland in March 2009, with two British soldiers and a PSNI officer being shot dead over a forty-eight-hour period. Dissident republicans, opposed to the peace process and the Good Friday Agreement, admitted responsibility for the attacks, which were the latest in a series of near-fatal shootings and bombings dating back to November 2007. Since then numerous incidents, including the shooting and wounding of two off-duty police officers in November 2007, the firing of Rocket Propelled Grenades (RPGs), the detonation of several roadside bombs and landmines close to passing police patrols, and the under-publicised discovery of a 100-pound 'beer-keg' bomb in September 2008 have all pointed to both the capability and intent of militarists who remain unconvinced about the Sinn Féin 'peace strategy'. These latest acts represent the first killings of security personnel in a decade and the most deadly attacks by republican dissidents since the Omagh bombing of 1998. Yet, unlike the repatriation ceremonies that greeted soldiers who had fallen in foreign battle-fields in Iraq and Afghanistan, the two sappers cut down by automatic gunfire in Antrim were afforded no such honours, perhaps the starkest sign yet that Northern Ireland had become 'normalised'.

Security experts north and south of the border estimated that the groups in question, the Real Irish Republican Army (Real IRA) and the Continuity Irish Republican Army (CIRA), have around a hundred core members with around 200–300 people providing support. However, these memberships are believed to be extremely fluid and there is evidence that the groups are internally divided – the loyalties of Real IRA members, in particular, being split between the Omagh bombing suspects Michael McKevitt and Liam Campbell and a third leader in Derry. The two groups are also suspected of being heavily involved in criminal activities such as cross-border smuggling, racketeering, and prostitution – again, the CIRA, specifically, has been linked to factions involved in the so-called 'drugs war' in Limerick city. While over 100 people were convicted of membership of the organisations in the Republic following the Omagh bombing, no one received the maximum eight-year sentence, and the Gardaí – the Irish police – suspect that many of these are behind the latest escalation.[27]

The killings provoked outrage across the North, highlighted by the mass demonstrations such as the one organised by trade unions in Belfast city centre that attracted over 10,000 people. This public unity was reflected in the strong condemnations by the four church leaders and the First and Deputy First Ministers, with the one-time Derry IRA leader Martin McGuinness stating that:

> These people [the Real IRA] are the traitors to the island of Ireland; they have betrayed the political desires, hopes, and aspirations of all the people who live on this island.[28]

Amidst fears of loyalist reprisals, the loyalist community's political leaders met with Sinn Féin representatives – a symbolic and political gesture whose significance was described by a spokesman:

> We are going to meet the Lord Mayor of Belfast … we've never done this before. We've never been near Irish republicans or 'Shinners'. Everybody in Northern Ireland is reassessing their position, stepping up to the mark creating unity amongst all the people of Northern Ireland to stand against this evil … I wouldn't let them create any despair in our hearts or in our minds for achieving long-term peace.[29]

Despite the show of unity, the intelligence services and the local politicians remain deeply divided. In part, this is due to the reluctance by the DUP to accede to Sinn Féin's request for policing and justice responsibilities to be devolved to the Assembly; however, it is also related to Sinn Féin's embedded suspicion of MI5. This suspicion forms the basis of republicans' denunciations of the activities of 'securocrats' and their emphasis on loyalist–British collusion during the conflict. The *political* rationale for the division is to bolster the republican explanation of the conflict – recently referred to by one spokesman in the context of the debate over dealing with the past: 'The British government was the major protagonist in the conflict in Ireland. They therefore cannot be the objective facilitator of any truth recovery process.'[30]

These underlying tensions among the political elites belie the photo-op concord and betray potential popular unity. As one journalist has pointed out, unless intelligence services subject themselves to democratic accountability and unless the Stormont elites accept their democratic responsibilities, the response to the ongoing terrorist threat will remain ad hoc and subject to political factionalism.[31] Moreover, there does seem to be a touch of irony in Martin McGuinness' condemnation of these deadly attacks. After all, the one-time Derry IRA commander McGuinness allegedly authorised the escalation of the armed struggle in the early 1990s, including the obliteration of the British Army's Victor II checkpoint along the border with Donegal. One disillusioned former IRA volunteer, Anthony McIntyre, pointed to:

> Those of us who have 'been there and done that' and who can bear testimony to the utter futility of militarism look on events with a mixture of angst and guilt. Angst because of the lives being destroyed; guilt because the logic we preached in the Provisional IRA is their logic. Treading in our footsteps they will secure the same defeat, but for Martin McGuinness to denounce them as traitors for following the example he set for decades is to commit an act of treachery against truth.[32]

McIntyre's angst at the internal logic of Sinn Féin's 'peace strategy' is underpinned by the feeling among many former IRA volunteers that they have been betrayed by their erstwhile political masters. In the words of Ruairí Ó Brádaigh, the former President of Republican Sinn Féin, the political voice of the republican dissidents:

> I have always said that anyone with an acquaintance with Irish history would realise what happens. Ireland was invaded by England and colonised and this was met with resistance. That resistance has been the way for hundreds of years. So I would feel that what happened last weekend could have happened and will happen at any time.[33]

There is little doubt that dissident republicans will remain, for some time to come, a potent and deadly threat to the peace process.

Learning and sharing the lessons of the conflict

In the decade between 1997 and May 2007, Northern Ireland experienced forty months of power sharing.[34] Following the agreement by Sinn Féin and the DUP to share power in May 2007, the executive did not meet for a further five months owing to the stand-off over the devolution of policing and justice. As we have pointed out in previous chapters, the Agreement provided for a fragile system of conflict management, but has done little to provide for any semblance of good government in Northern Ireland. During much of those first ten years, for example, Sinn Féin's political agenda was centred on maximising gains from the British government in return for decommissioning. The 'choreography' has often made these links explicit: in 2001 legislation on police reform followed an act of decommissioning; again, the passing of the 2003 Police Act followed movement on the issue.[35] This process had deleterious effects on the 'middle-ground' parties, the SDLP and the UUP. The latter, in particular, suffered from a drastic loss of public confidence, with many of its traditional supporters simply refusing to turn out at successive general and Assembly elections, leaving the path clear for the accession of the DUP, first in 2003 and again in 2005.[36]

Quite why Tony Blair continued to acquiesce to republicans following the international consensus on facing down terrorism after 9/11; or the revelations of a republican 'spy-ring' in the Assembly in 2003; or the evidence of IRA involvement in the robbery of £26 million from the Northern Bank in Belfast in 2004 and the savage killing of a Catholic in a city centre bar in 2005 remains largely unknown. However, Blair's chief-of-staff inadvertently hinted at what might be a plausible answer, 'perhaps the most important change of all was in the attitude of the British government':

> Sometimes ... a certain amount of political pain is unavoidable to keep the process going ... We carried on because we understood the battle that Adams and McGuinness were facing in their attempts to win over the Republican movement ... Previous British governments had tried to split the IRA in order to defeat it and had enjoyed some success. But we wanted to make peace only once, rather than many times, and above all we wanted to keep the Provisional IRA together rather than letting it be replaced by yet another capable republican terrorist group.[37]

Following the recent attacks by republican dissidents, Powell reiterated his conclusions but added the further lesson that the British media should not give the splinter groups attention; unfortunately, he did not elaborate on how car bombs and dead bodies can be 'spun' out of existence.[38]

Powell's dilemma illustrates the intellectual and moral vacuity of what we have referred to as the peace process industry. This industry depends upon standardising and propagating certain 'lessons' about the Northern Ireland conflict. An intellectual deficit arises from the occasions when the sharing of 'lessons' has little to do with the actual historical record. In fact those 'lessons' are often either wilful manipulation of the historical record or are confounded by the persistence of political division. Underpinning this conceit is a moral vacuum based on unexamined platitudes such as the belief that political power must be divided out according to ethnic head-counts and with little regard to principles of democratic accountability or responsibility. Another example is the growing call for Northern Irish society to be forcibly reconciled, regardless of the fact that the vast majority of people consistently repudiated terrorist violence.

Despite the tendency of the peace process industry towards monopoly, we are confident that the platitudes and the conceits upon which it is based and which it recycles are time-bound. The availability of archival sources, upon which this book is based, forms the basis of a new revisionist model that stresses empirical criticism and theoretical reflection, and which is being shaped by young political scientists and experienced historians – this book has drawn on many of these innovative insights.[39] The second reason that we are confident that the old narratives will not shape the future of Northern Ireland is the fact that a new generation of young adults is taking its place in the public sphere, for whom the old stories will not stand. In this view, the logic of the consociational structures risks losing a certain popular legitimacy insofar as young voters who knew nothing of the Troubles will be less willing to buy in to the pragmatic and deeply compromised politics of the past.

Further reading

General histories

The general background and events of the Northern Ireland conflict are found in Paul Bew, *Ireland: The Politics of Enmity, 1789–2006* (Oxford: Oxford University Press, 2007); R.F. Foster, *Modern Ireland, 1600–1972* (London: Penguin, 1989); Alvin Jackson, *Home Rule: An Irish History, 1800–2000* (London: Weidenfeld & Nicolson, 2003); and Henry Patterson, *Ireland since 1939: The Persistence of Conflict* (Dublin: Penguin, 2006).

Histories of the Northern Irish state include Paul Bew, Peter Gibbon, and Henry Patterson, *Northern Ireland 1921–2001: Political Forces and Social Classes* (London: Serif, 2002) and Thomas Hennessey, *A History of Northern Ireland: 1921–1996* (Dublin: Gill & Macmillan, 1997); Brendan O'Leary and John McGarry's *The Politics of Antagonism: Understanding Northern Ireland* (London: Athlone Press, 1996) provides a political science perspective on the state.

Although the conflict itself gave rise to a wealth of academic literature, the fact that it remained ongoing until recently, together with the unavailability of archival material meant that there are few general histories. Paul Dixon's *Northern Ireland: The Politics of War and Peace* (Basingstoke: Palgrave, 2001) and Cillian McGrattan's *Northern Ireland, 1968–2008: The Politics of Entrenchment* (Basingstoke: Palgrave Macmillan, forthcoming) provide critical overviews of the conflict.

Rosemary Sales, *Women Divided: Gender, Religion and Politics in Northern Ireland* (London: Routledge, 1997) offers a corrective to the male-dominated politics and historiography of Northern Ireland. Jonathan Tonge's *The New Northern Irish Politics?* (Basingstoke: Palgrave Macmillan, 2005) also provides an accessible analysis of the actions and aspirations of the main contending groups.

In many ways, the most important and unsettling text relating to the conflict is *Lost Lives: The Stories of the Men, Women, and Children Who Died as a Result of the Northern Ireland Troubles*, by David McKittrick, Seamus Kelters, Brian Feeney, and Chris Thornton (Edinburgh: Mainstream, 2004). Paul Bew and Gordon Gillespie's *Northern Ireland: A Chronology of the Troubles, 1966–1999* (Dublin: Gill & Macmillan, 1999) serves as a key reference text.

The two crucial texts on the Northern Irish peace process are Dean Godson's *Himself Alone: David Trimble and the Ordeal of Unionism* (London: HarperCollins, 2004); and Eamonn O'Kane's *Britain, Ireland and Northern Ireland since 1980: The Totality of Relationships* (London: Routledge, 2007). Kirk Simpson's *Truth Recovery in Northern Ireland: Critically Interpreting the Past* (Manchester: Manchester University Press, 2009) is a key intervention in the emerging debate over the meaning of the Troubles.

Party histories

Sinn Féin and the IRA have been the subject of several discerning books: Rogelio Alonso, *The IRA and the Armed Struggle* (London: Routledge, 2007); Kevin Bean, *The New Politics of Sinn Féin* (Liverpool: Liverpool University Press, 2007); Martyn Frampton, *The Long March: The Political Strategy of Sinn Féin, 1981–2007* (Basingstoke: Palgrave Macmillan, 2009); and Henry Patterson, *The Politics of Illusion: A Political History of the IRA* (London: Serif, 1997).

Richard English's *Irish Freedom: The History of Nationalism in Ireland* (London: Macmillan, 2006) is a key text for anyone interested in Irish nationalism, while Gerard Murray's *John Hume and the SDLP: Impact and Survival in Northern Ireland* (Dublin: Irish Academic Press, 1998) provides a critical history of the SDLP.

Catherine O'Donnell's *Fianna Fáil, Irish Republicanism and the Northern Ireland Troubles, 1968–2005* (Dublin: Irish Academic Press, 2007) is the most authoritative study of the Irish state's role in the conflict; while Michael Cunningham's *British Government Policy in Northern Ireland, 1969–2000* (Manchester: Manchester University Press, 2001) focuses on the role of successive Westminster governments in the North.

As is the case with republican politics, readers with an interest in Ulster unionism have been well served in recent years by several essential texts, including Arthur Aughey, *Under Siege: Ulster Unionism and the Anglo-Irish Agreement* (London: Hurst, 1989); Christopher Farrington, *Ulster Unionism and the Peace Process* (Basingstoke: Palgrave, 2006); Henry Patterson and Eric Kaufmann, *Unionism and Orangeism since 1945: The Decline of the Loyal Family* (Manchester: Manchester University Press, 2007); and Graham Walker, *A History of the Ulster Unionist Party: Protest, Pragmatism, and Pessimism* (Manchester: Manchester University Press, 2004).

Recent texts on loyalism include Peter Taylor's *Loyalists* (London: Bloomsbury, 2000) and Ian Wood's *Crimes of Loyalty: A History of the UDA* (Edinburgh: Edinburgh University Press, 2006).

Readers interested in labour history should consult Aaron Edwards' *A History of the Northern Ireland Labour Party: Democratic Socialism and Sectarianism* (Manchester: Manchester University Press, 2009), and Belinda Probert's *Beyond Orange and Green: The Political Economy of the Northern Ireland Crisis* (Dublin: Academy Press, 1978).

Political memoirs

Garret FitzGerald's *All in a Life* (London: Macmillan, 1991); John Major's *John Major: The Autobiography* (London: HarperCollins, 1999); and Margaret Thatcher's *The Downing Street Years* (London: HarperCollins, 1993) provide detailed accounts of each premier's time in office. Merlyn Rees's *Northern Ireland: A Personal Perspective* (London: Methuen, 1985) and Jonathan Powell's *Great Hatred, Little Room: Making Peace in Northern Ireland* (The Bodley Head, 2008) also provide insiders' accounts of the British policymaking process. Sir Kenneth Bloomfield's *A Tragedy of Errors: The Government and Misgovernment of Northern Ireland* (Liverpool: Liverpool University Press, 2007) builds on his own experiences at the heart of the British policymaking apparatus to deliver a sometimes damning critique of government intervention.

Gerry Adams' series of autobiographies – *Before the Dawn: An Autobiography* (London: Heinemann, 1996); *Hope and History: Making Peace in Ireland* (Dingle: Brandon, 2005) – provide a unique perspective on the republican experience; while Austin Currie's *All Hell Will Break Loose* (Dublin: O'Brien Press, 2004) and Paddy Devlin's *Straight Left: An Autobiography* (Belfast: Blackstaff, 1993) offer insights into the SDLP's politics.

Brian Faulkner's *Memoirs of a Statesman* (London: Weidenfeld and Nicolson, 1978) remains one of only a limited number of autobiographies by a unionist leader, although Basil McIvor's *Hope Deferred: Experiences of an Irish Unionist* (Belfast: Blackstaff, 1998) provides insights into 'backbench' unionist politics during the 1970s and 1980s.

Endnotes

Introduction

1. The April 1998 Agreement provided for a devolved administration in Northern Ireland, elected through proportional representation, and headed by an executive that would be drawn from the main unionist and nationalist political representatives. It also provided for cross-border cooperation in a number of social and economic areas and for extensive review of the criminal justice system, including the early release of paramilitary prisoners. While the document was simply termed 'the Agreement', unionists have come to use the prefix 'Belfast' while nationalists have preferred 'Good Friday' – a division that is often taken as symbolically representative of the different ways in which the Agreement has been open to interpretation.
2. O'Leary, Brendan and John McGarry, *The Politics of Antagonism: Understanding Northern Ireland* (London: Athlone Press, 1997), p. 12.
3. For statistics and details on Troubles-related deaths, see McKittrick, David, Seamus Kelters, Brian Feeney, and Chris Thornton, *Lost Lives: The Stories of the Men, Women, and Children Who Died as a Result of the Northern Ireland Troubles* (Edinburgh: Mainstream, 2004).
4. Kaldor, Mary, *Old and New Wars* (Cambridge: Polity, 2006).

Chapter 1

1. Ferguson, Niall, *Empire: How Britain Made the Modern World* (London: Penguin, 2004), p. 315.

2. Edwards, Aaron, *A History of the Northern Ireland Labour Party: Democratic Socialism and Sectarianism* (Manchester: Manchester University Press, 2009).

3. Cited in Bew, Paul, *Ireland: The Politics of Enmity* (Oxford: Oxford University Press, 2008), p. 382.

4. McGrattan, Cillian, *Northern Ireland, 1968–2008: The Politics of Entrenchment* (Basingstoke: Palgrave Macmillan, forthcoming).

5. Phoenix, Eamon, *Northern Nationalism: Nationalist Politics, Partition, and the Catholic Minority in Northern Ireland, 1890–1940* (Belfast: Ulster Historical Society, 1994), p. 399.

6. Bew, Paul, Peter Gibbon, and Henry Patterson, *Northern Ireland, 1921–2001: Political Forces and Social Classes* (London: Serif, 2002), pp. 49–55.

7. Lynch, Robert 'The people's protectors? The Irish Republican Army and the "Belfast Pogrom", 1920–1922', *Journal of British Studies*, 47 (April 2008), 375.

8. Edwards, *A History of the Northern Ireland Labour Party*, p. 19.

9. Patterson, Henry, *Ireland since 1939: The Persistence of Conflict* (London: Penguin Books, 2007), pp. 43–4.

10. Edwards, Aaron, 'Abandoning armed resistance? The Ulster Volunteer Force as a case-study of strategic terrorism in Northern Ireland', *Studies in Conflict and Terrorism*, 32 (2) (February 2009), 146–66.

11. Bodleian Library Special Collections (hereafter BLSC), *Clement Attlee Papers*, MS. Attlee Dep. 37, Fols. 89–90. 'Message from Clement Attlee to Flying-Officer Desmond Donnelly, 30 May 1946'.

12. BLSC, *Clement Attlee Papers*, MS. Attlee Dep. 82, Fol. 182., 'Secret – Ireland Bill: Northern Ireland Election'.

13. BLSC, *Clement Attlee Papers*, MS. Attlee Dep. 82, Fols. 256–8, 'Confidential – Ireland Bill: Partition Question'.

14. Lord Brookeborough speaking at Stormont during a debate on recent IRA attacks. 18 December 1956, Northern Ireland Parliamentary Debates: Official Report, Vol. 40, Col. 3208.

15. *The Times*, 15 December 1956.

16. Edwards, *A History of the Northern Ireland Labour Party*.

17. Quoted in Patterson, Henry and Eric Kaufmann, *Unionism and Orangeism in Northern Ireland since 1945: The Decline of the Loyal Family* (Manchester: Manchester University Press, 2007), p. 57.

18. Many of these statistics have been taken from the Campaign for Social Justice's (1969) booklet, 'Northern Ireland: The Plain Truth', available at www.cain.ulst.ac.uk.

19. Patterson, *Ireland*, p. 198.

20. McKittrick, David and David McVea, *Making Sense of the Troubles* (London: Penguin, 2001), p. 25.

21. Currie, Austin, 'Caledon was about forcing the British to address injustices in the North', *Irish News*, 21 June 2008.

22. Bew, *Ireland*, p. 493.

23. McCormack, Vincent, 'Route '68: to Burntollet and back', *History Ireland*, September 2008.

24. Edwards, Aaron, 'Social democracy and partition: the British Labour Party and Northern Ireland, 1951–64', *Journal of Contemporary History*, 42 (4), (October 2007), 595–612.

25. Craig, F.W.S., *Conservative and Labour Party Conference Decisions, 1945–1981* (Chichester: Parliamentary Research Services, 1982), p. 422.

26. Hennessey, Thomas, *Northern Ireland: The Origins of the Troubles* (Dublin: Gill & Macmillan, 2005).

27. Shanahan, Timothy, *The Provisional IRA and the Morality of Terrorism* (Edinburgh: Edinburgh University Press, 2009), p. 22.

28. Patterson, Henry, *The Politics of Illusion: A Political History of the IRA* (London: Serif, 1997), p. 128.

29. National Archives of the United Kingdom, Kew (henceforth NA), FCO 26/990, 'Implications of Northern Ireland for British Foreign Policy, 11 February 1972'.

30. Hennessey, Thomas, *The Evolution of the Troubles, 1970–72* (Dublin: Gill & Macmillan, 2007).

31. Shanahan, *The Provisional IRA*, p. 28; emphasis in the original.

32. *Irish Independent*, 11 March 1972.

33. *Belfast Newsletter*, 7 March 1972.

34. Ibid.

35. Edwards, *A History of the Northern Ireland Labour Party*.

36. BLSC, Wilson Papers, Col. 908, Fol. 213, Harold Wilson to Conor Cruise O'Brien, dated April 1972.

37. *Sunday Independent*, 12 March 1972.

38. Walker, Graham, *A History of the Ulster Unionist Party* (Manchester: Manchester University Press, 2004), p. 212.

39. Cited in ibid. p. 213.

40. Walker, Graham, 'The Protestant working class and the fragmentation of Ulster Unionism', in Mervyn Busteed, Frank Neal, and Jonathan Tonge (eds), *Irish Protestant Identities* (Manchester: Manchester University Press, 2008), pp. 360–72.

Chapter 2

1. *Sunday News*, 9 April 1972.

2. Whitelaw, William, *The Whitelaw Memoirs* (London: Aurum, 1989), p. 100.

3. *Belfast Newsletter*, 27 February 1973.

4. Patterson, Henry, 'Brian Faulkner', *Dictionary of National Biography*, 2008.

5. Kennedy, Lindsay, 'Diary entry, 1 October 1973', Public Record Office of Northern Ireland (PRONI) D/4175/4/31/1.

6. *Irish Independent*, 25 May 1972.

7. Devlin, Paddy, *Straight Left: An Autobiography* (Belfast: Blackstaff, 1993), p. 183.

8. SDLP, *Towards a New Ireland*, available at www.cain.ulst.ac.uk.

9. 'SDLP Proposals, 21 September 1972', National Archives of Ireland (Dublin) (henceforth NAI) DFA/2004/7/2698.

10. 'Council of Ireland, Paper 1', N.D. [December 1972], NAI DT/2003/16/430.

11. 'Memorandum on the conference proposed by the British government's White Paper', 24 May 1973, NAI DT/2004/21/624.

12. *Belfast Newsletter*, 3 October 1973.

13. Quoted in McGrattan, Cillian, 'Dublin, the SDLP and the Sunningdale Agreement: maximalist nationalism and path dependency', *Contemporary British History*, 23 (1), (2009).

14. See, for example, the famous Christmas dinner exchange in *The Portrait of the Artist as a Young Man,* in James Joyce, *A James Joyce Reader* (London: Penguin, 1993), pp. 268–83; or 'Ivy Day in the Committee Room', in *Dubliners* (London: Paladin, 1988 [1914]).

15. Hume opens the chapter in his autobiography on 'British policy in Ireland' with Parnell's phrase, 'No man has the right to fix the boundary of the march of a nation'; the following chapter deals with 'The Unionist heritage'; see John Hume, *Personal Views: Politics, Peace, and Reconciliation in Ireland* (Dublin: Town House, 1996), pp. 33–62.

16. Murray, Gerard, *John Hume and the SDLP: Impact and Survival in Northern Ireland* (Dublin: Irish Academic Press, 1998), p. 256.

17. Bew, Paul and Gordon Gillespie, *Northern Ireland: A Chronology of the Troubles, 1968–1999* (Dublin: Gill & Macmillan), p. 63.

18. *Belfast Newsletter*, 20 November 1973.

19. *Belfast Newsletter*, 28 November 1973.

20. Faulkner, Brian, *Memoirs of a Statesman* (London: Weidenfeld & Nicolson, 1978), p. 193.

21. McIvor, Basil, *Experiences of an Irish Unionist* (Belfast: Blackstaff Press, 1998), pp. 101–2.

22. Bew, *Ireland*, p. 512.

23. Faulkner, *Memoirs*, p. 222.

24. *Belfast Newsletter*, 12 December 1973.

25. 'McLachlan telephone call, 4 January 1974', NAI DT/2005/7/624.

26. 'Note for the record, meeting between Brian Faulkner and Frank Cooper', 5 March 1974, NA CJ 4/786.

27. 'Prime Minister's meeting with Rt Hon. Brian Faulkner, 1 April 1974', NA PREM 16/163.

28. Rees to Wilson, 8 April 1974, NA CJ 4/473.

29. 'Sunningdale: alternative courses of action, 26 March 1974', NAI DT/2005/7/658.

30. 'Summary report of meeting between SDLP and the Irish government, 29 April 1974', NAI DT/2005/7/649.

31. Hume, *Personal Views* pp. 38–9.

32. Ibid., pp. 29–30.

33. Faulkner, *Memoirs*, p. 282.

34. Kerr, Michael, *Imposing Power-Sharing: Conflict and Co-Existence in Northern Ireland and Lebanon* (Dublin: Irish Academic Press, 2007), p. 62.

Chapter 3

1. Rees to Wilson, 31 May 1974, NA PREM 16/148.

2. Haines, Joe, *The Politics of Power* (London: Cape, 1977), p. 133.

3. Bew, Paul and Henry Patterson, *The British State and the Ulster Crisis: From Wilson to Thatcher* (London: Verso, 1985), p. 77.

4. Donoughue, Bernard, *The Heat of the Kitchen: An Autobiography* (London: Pimlico's, 2003), p. 137.

5. Note by the Northern Ireland Office (to the British Cabinet), February 1975, NA CJ 4/753.

6. Donoughue to Wilson, 'Northern Ireland: Future policy options, 21 September 1975', NA PREM 16/520.

7. Donoughue, *Heat*, pp. 135–8.

8. O'Leary and McGarry, *The Politics of Antagonism*.

9. *The Northern Ireland Constitution* (London: Her Majesty's Stationery Office, 1974), paragraph 45.

10. 'The political situation in Northern Ireland', NA CJ 4/492.

11. *Irish News*, 29 December 2006.

12. Patterson and Kaufmann, *Unionism*, p. 180.

13. Maurice Hayes, 'Conversation with Dr Paisley, 11 September 1975', PRONI CONV/1/2.

14. Cubbon to Janes, 22 June 1976, NA CJ 4/1440.
15. 'Machinery of Government, Note by the NIO', 29 April 1975, NA CJ 4/755.
16. 'Distancing, Note by the NIO', July 1975, NA CJ 4/756.
17. *Irish Times*, 29 December 2005.
18. Bew and Patterson, *British State*, pp. 80–1.
19. White, Robert W., *Ruairí Ó Brádaigh: The Life and Politics of an Irish Revolutionary* (Chesham: Indiana University Press, 2006), p. 220.
20. *Guardian*, 18 March 2008.
21. Wilson, 'Apocalyptic note for the record, 10 January 1976', NA CJ 4/1358.
22. Hunt to Wilson, 16 January 1976, NA PREM 16/690.
23. *Irish Times*, 28 December 2007.
24. *The Telegraph*, 18 May 2004.
25. *Irish Times*, 28 September 1976.
26. Hennessey, Thomas, *A History of Northern Ireland: 1920–1996* (Basingstoke: Palgrave, 1997), p. 238; O'Leary and McGarry, *The Politics of Antagonism*, pp. 206–8
27. O'Leary and McGarry, *The Politics of Antagonism*, pp. 208–9.
28. Alonso, Ropelio, *The IRA and Armed Struggle* (London: Routledge, 2007), p. 67.
29. O'Rawe, Richard, *Blanketmen: An Untold Story of the H-Block Hunger Strike* (Dublin: New Island, 2005), pp. 176–83.
30. FitzGerald, Garret, *All in a Life: An Autobiography* (London: Macmillan, 1991) p. 463.
31. O'Kane, Eamonn, *Britain, Ireland, and Northern Ireland since 1980: The Totality of Relationships* (Abingdon: Routledge, 2007), p. 40.
32. Farrell, John A., *Tip O'Neill and the Democratic Century* (Boston: Little, Brown & Company, 2001), pp. 222–4.
33. Thatcher, Margaret, *The Downing Street Years* (London: HarperCollins, 1993), p. 385.
34. O'Kane, *Britain*, p. 193.
35. Bew, *Ireland*, p. 532.

Chapter 4

1. McGrattan, Cillian, 'Northern Nationalism and the Belfast Agreement', in Barton, Brian and Patrick J. Roche (eds) *The Northern Ireland Question: The Peace Process and the Belfast Agreement* (Basingstoke: Palgrave, 2009), pp. 156–9.

2. O'Leary and McGarry, *The Politics of Antagonism*.

3. McGrattan, Cillian, 'Learning from the past or laundering history? Consociational narratives and British state intervention in Northern Ireland', *British Politics*, 5(1), (2010).

4. Hume, *Personal Views*, p. 46.

5. Murray, Gerard, and Jonathan Tonge, *Sinn Féin and the SDLP: from Alienation to Participation* (Dublin: O'Brien Press, 2005), p. 173.

6. Ibid., p. 52.

7. Bew et al., *Northern Ireland*, p. 210.

8. O'Kane, Eamonn, 'Re-evaluating the Anglo-Irish Agreement: central or incidental to the Northern Ireland Peace Process?', *International Politics*, 44, (2007), 714.

9. Moloney, Ed, *A Secret History of the IRA* (London: Penguin, 2003), p. 245.

10. Bean, Kevin, *The New Politics of Sinn Féin* (Liverpool: Liverpool University Press, 2007).

11. Patterson, *Politics*, pp. 313–14.

12. Moloney, *History*, pp. 251–2.

13. McGrattan, 'Northern Nationalism', p. 157.

14. Murray and Tonge, *Sinn Féin*, p.166.

15. Challengers to the Adams camp included Ruairí Ó Brádaigh, Daithi O'Conaill, and Ivor Bell. See McIntyre, Anthony, 'Of myths and men: dissent within Republicanism and Loyalism', in Aaron Edwards and Stephen Bloomer (eds), *Transforming the Peace Process in Northern Ireland: From Terrorism to Democratic Politics* (Dublin: Irish Academic Press, 2008), p. 121.

16. Cited in McGrattan, Cillian, 'Modern Irish Nationalism: ideology, policymaking and path-dependent change', in Adrian Guelke

(ed.), *The Challenges of Ethno-Nationalism: Case Studies in Identity Politics* (Basingstoke: Palgrave Macmillan, forthcoming).

17. Freedman, Lawrence, 'Reconciling the incompatible', *The Times*, 20 November 1993.

18. 'Six County Internal Conference, 25 June 1988', Linenhall Library, Northern Ireland Political Collection, Tom Hartley Papers.

19. Oppenheimer, A.R., *IRA, the Bombs and the Bullets: A History of Deadly Ingenuity* (Dublin: Irish Academic Press, 2009), p. 135.

20. 'Passing the hat for the Provos', *Time Magazine*, 26 November 1979.

21. Guelke, Adrian, 'The United States, Irish Americans and the Northern Ireland Peace Process', *International Affairs*, 72 (3), (July 1996), 521–36.

22. McDonald, Henry, *Gunsmoke and Mirrors: How Sinn Féin Dressed Up Defeat as Victory* (Dublin: Gill & Macmillan, 2008), p. 157.

23. Powell, Jonathan, *Great Hatred, Little Room: Making Peace in Northern Ireland* (London: The Bodley Head, 2008), pp. 12–13, 79–80.

24. *An Phoblacht/Republican News*, 23 April 1998.

25. Ibid.

26. Tonge, Jonathan, *The New Northern Irish Politics* (Basingstoke: Palgrave, 2006), p. 262.

27. Alonso, *The IRA*, p. 148.

28. Cited in ibid, p. 148.

29. *Irish News*, 6 October 2006.

30. Shirlow, Peter and Brendan Murtagh, *Belfast: Segregation, Violence, and the City* (London: Pluto, 2006).

31. Edwards, Aaron, 'Drawing a line under the past', *Peace Review: A Journal of Social Justice*, 20 (2), (April–June 2008), 209–17.

Chapter 5

1. NICVA, *State of the Sector V* (Belfast: NICVA, 2008).
2. Edwards interview with Stephen Bloomer, 20 January 2009.

3. Lederach, 'From Truce to Transformation'.

4. Lederach, John Paul, 'From Truce to Transformation', address to the Live Issues 5 Conference, Wellington Park Hotel, 23 November 2007. Archived at: http://soap2.tibus.com/communityrelations_new/filestore/documents/Truce_to_Transformation.pdf. Accessed: 23 February 2009.

5. The Agreement reached at multi-party talks on 10 April 1998.

6. Edwards interview with Michael Doherty, Derry/Londonderry, 18 December 2008.

7. Jarman, Neil, 'Ordering transition', in Aaron Edwards and Stephen Bloomer (eds), *Transforming the Peace Process in Northern Ireland: From Terrorism to Democratic Politics* (Dublin: Irish Academic Press, 2008), p. 135.

8. Edwards interview with Syd Trotter, Belfast, 16 December 2008.

9. Steadman, Stephen J., 'Spoiler problems in peace processes', *International Security*, 22(2), (Fall 1997), 5–53.

10. Edwards interview with Nigel Gardiner, Derry/Londonderry, 18 December 2008.

11. Edwards interview with Syd Trotter, Belfast, 16 December 2008.

12. Wood, Ian S., *Crimes of Loyalty: A History of the Ulster Defence Association* (Edinburgh: Edinburgh University Press, 2006), p. 256.

13. *The Times*, 23 November 2000.

14. *Belfast Newsletter*, 3 August 2002.

15. Edwards interview with Syd Trotter, Belfast, 16 December 2008.

16. Edwards interview with Catherine Cooke, Derry/Londonderry, 19 December 2008.

17. McIntyre, Anthony, 'Provisional Republicanism: internal politics, inequalities and modes of repression', in Fearghal McGarry (ed.), *Republicanism in Modern Ireland* (Dublin: University College Dublin Press, 2003), p. 183.

18. McIntyre, 'Dissent within Republicanism and Loyalism', in Edwards and Bloomer, *Transforming the Peace Process*.

19. McIntyre, Anthony, *Good Friday: The Death of Irish Republicanism* (New York: Ausubo Press, 2008), p. 152.

20. Ibid., p. 3.
21. Bean, *Sinn Féin*, p. 217.
22. Edwards interview with Catherine Cooke, Derry/Londonderry, 19 December 2008.
23. *Derry Journal*, 4 March 2009.
24. Edwards interview with Michael Doherty, Derry/Londonderry, 18 December 2008.
25. Edwards interview with Catherine Cooke, Derry/Londonderry, 19 December 2008.
26. *Derry Journal*, 26 February 2008.
27. Edwards interview with Syd Trotter, Belfast, 16 December 2008.
28. Edwards interview with Nigel Gardiner, Derry/Londonderry, 18 December 2008.
29. Bean, *Sinn Féin*, pp. 220–1.
30. Edwards 'Drawing a line under the past'.
31. Edwards interview with Michael Doherty, Derry/Londonderry, 18 December 2008.
32. Edwards interview with Michael Doherty, Derry/Londonderry, 18 December 2008.
33. Edwards interview with Syd Trotter, Belfast, 16 December 2008.
34. Edwards interview with Harry Donaghy, Belfast, 16 December 2008.
35. Edwards interview with Catherine Cooke, Derry/Londonderry, 19 December 2008.
36. Edwards interview with Nigel Gardiner, Derry/Londonderry, 18 December 2008.

Chapter 6

1. McGrattan, Cillian, '"Explaining Northern Ireland?" The limitations of the ethnic conflict model', *National Identities*, forthcoming.
2. See O'Leary and McGarry, *Politics*; McGarry, John and Brendan O'Leary, *Explaining Northern Ireland: Broken Images* (Oxford:

Blackwell, 2000). McGarry and O'Leary's students continue to reproduce variations on the theme: see Kerr, *Imposing Power-Sharing*; and O'Duffy, Brendan, *British–Irish Relations and Northern Ireland: From Violent Politics to Conflict Regulation* (Dublin: Irish Academic Press, 2008).

3. Shirlow, Peter and Kieran McEvoy, *Beyond the Wire: Former Prisoners and Conflict Transformation in Northern Ireland* (London: Pluto, 2008), p. 1.

4. Bruce, Steve, *Paisley* (Oxford: Oxford University Press, 2007), p. 246.

5. Mitchell, Claire, *Religion, Identity and Politics in Northern Ireland: Boundaries of Belonging and Belief* (Aldershot: Ashgate, 2006).

6. Alonso, *The IRA*, pp. 15–16.

7. Introductory texts include Aretxaga, Begoña, *Shattering Silence: Women, Nationalism, and Political Subjectivity in Northern Ireland* (Princeton: Princeton University Press, 1997); Ashe, Fidelma, 'Gender and ethno-nationalist politics', in Coulter, Colin and Martin Murray, *Northern Ireland after the Troubles: A Society in Transition* (Manchester: Manchester University Press, 2008); and Roulston, Carmel, and Celia Davies, *Gender, Democracy and Inclusion in Northern Ireland* (Basingstoke: Palgrave, 2000).

8. Zalewski, Marysia, 'Gender ghosts in McGarry and O'Leary and representations of the conflict in Northern Ireland', *Political Studies*, 53 (1), (2005), 201–21.

9. McDowell, Sara, 'Commemorating dead "men": gendering the past and present in post-conflict Northern Ireland', *Gender, Place and Culture*, 15 (4), (2008), 338.

10. Ashe, Fidelma, 'Iris Robinson's excitable speech: sexuality and conflict transformation in Northern Ireland', *Politics*, 29 (1), (2009), 23. Robinson had described homosexuality as 'disgusting, loathsome, nauseating, shamefully wicked', and 'an abomination'.

11. Ashe, 'Gender', p. 163.

12. Edwards interview with Catherine Cooke, Derry/Londonderry, 19 December 2008.

13. Laitin, David D., *Nations, States and Violence* (Oxford: Oxford University Press, 2007).

14. Darby, John and Roger MacGinty, *Guns and Government: The Management of the Northern Ireland Peace Process* (Basingstoke: Palgrave, 2002), p. 21.

15. McGrattan, 'Learning from the past'.

16. Kerr, *Imposing*, p. 41.

17. McGrattan, 'Learning from the past'.

18. Taylor, Rupert, 'The Belfast Agreement and the limitations of consociationalism', in Christopher Farrington (ed.), *Global Change, Civil Society and the Northern Ireland Peace Process: Implementing the Political Settlement* (Basingstoke: Palgrave Macmillan, 2008).

19. McGarry and O'Leary, *Explaining*.

Conclusion

1. Shirlow, Peter and Brendan Murtagh, *Belfast: Segregation, Violence, and the City* (London: Pluto, 2006).

2. Jarman, Neil, *No Longer a Problem? Sectarian Violence in Northern Ireland* (Belfast: Institute for Conflict Research, 2005), www.conflictresearch.org.uk/documents/violence.pdf.

3. Shirlow and Murtagh, *Belfast*, pp. 52–5.

4. *Irish Times*, 28 January, 2000.

5. Mitchell, Paul, Brendan O'Leary, and Geoffrey Evans, 'Northern Ireland: flanking extremists bite the moderates and emerge in their clothes', *Parliamentary Affairs*, 54 (4), (2001), 725–42.

6. *Irish Times*, 9 March 2008.

7. Shirlow and Murtagh, *Belfast*.

8. McDowell, Sara, 'Commemorating dead "men" ', p. 340.

9. Edwards, 'Drawing a line under the past'; McGrattan, Cillian, '"Order out of chaos": the politics of transitional justice', *Politics*, 29 (3), (2009), 164–72.

10. *Irish Times*, 25 October 1997.

11. 'We Will Remember Them', Report of the Northern Ireland Victims Commissioner, Sir Kenneth Bloomfield, KCB (Belfast: The Stationery Office, 1998), available online at www.nio.gov. uk/bloomfield_report.pdf.

12. *Belfast Telegraph*, 22 June 2007.

13. Consultative Group on the Past, *Report of the Consultative Group on the Past* (Belfast, 2009), available online at www.cgpni.org.

14. McBride, Patricia, (Victims Commissioner), *Belfast Telegraph*, 30 January 2009. See McGrattan, 'Dublin, the SDLP and the Sunningdale Agreement'.

15. Patterson, Henry, 'Truth and reconciliation in Northern Ireland? Not much hope of either', *Parliamentary Brief*, February 2009; McGrattan '"Order out of chaos"'.

16. *Irish Times*, 29 January 2008.

17. Breen-Smyth, Marie, *Truth Recovery and Justice after Conflict; Managing Violent Pasts* (London: Routledge, 2007).

18. Ex-Prisoners' Interpretive Centre (EPIC), *Truth Recovery: A Contribution from Loyalism* (Belfast: EPIC, 2004), p. 9.

19. Evans, Richard, *In Hitler's Shadow: West German Historians and the Attempt to Escape from the Nazi Past* (London: Tauris, 1989), p. 40.

20. Sinn Féin, *Truth: A Sinn Féin Discussion Document* (Belfast: Sinn Féin, 2003), p. 4.

21. Northern Ireland Affairs Committee, *Ways of Dealing with Northern Ireland's Past: Interim Report – Victims and Survivors* (London: The Stationery Office, 2005).

22. McEvoy, Kieran, *Making Peace with the Past* (Belfast: Healing Through Remembering, 2006), p. 80.

23. O'Toole, Fintan, 'Sinn Féin's silence on IRA killing', *Irish Times*, 28 June 2005; see also Morrison, Danny, 'Dirty fighting', *Guardian*, 13 January 2009.

24. EPIC, *Truth recovery*.

25. Adorno, Theodor, 'The meaning of working through the past', in R. Tiedeman (ed.), *Can One Live after Auschwitz?* (Stanford: Stanford University Press, 2003).

26. Feeney, Brian, 'Assembly is powerless when it comes to finance', *Irish News*, 8 October 2008.

27. See 'Dissident chiefs "addicted" to criminality', *Irish Times*, 12 March 2009; 'Splintered republican dissident groups are difficult to penetrate', *Irish Times*, 11 March 2009; *Six-One*, RTÉ One, 12 March 2009.

28. 'McGuinness: "These people are traitors"', on BBC News online, 10 March 2009; available at http://news.bbc.co.uk/1/hi/northern_ireland/7934894.stm, accessed 6 October 2009.

29. Frankie Gallagher, *Irish Times*, 12 March 2009.

30. Gerry Kelly, cited in *The Irish News,* 21 February 2009.

31. Emerson, Newton, 'Accountability only way to draw out toxic intelligence', *Irish News*, 12 March 2009.

32. McIntyre, Anthony, 'Anthony McIntyre: who is McGuinness to talk of treachery?', *Independent on Sunday*, 15 March 2009.

33. Republican Sinn Féin President, Ruairí Ó Brádaigh, speaking to journalist Henry McDonald, 'As long as the British remain, there will always be some kind of IRA', *The Observer*, 15 March 2009.

34. Wilson, Robin, 'Common norms are what the North needs, not rival communities', *Irish Times*, 9 April 2008.

35. McGrattan, Cillian, *Northern Ireland, 1968–2008: The Politics of Entrenchment* (Basingstoke: Palgrave Macmillan).

36. For more on these changes, see Patterson, *Ireland*, pp. 339–58.

37. Powell, *Great Hatred,* pp. 312; 313–14.

38. Powell, Jonathan, 'These criminals can't hold the peace process hostage', *Guardian*, 10 March 2009.

39. English, Richard, *Irish Freedom: The History of Nationalism in Ireland* (London: Macmillan, 2006); Dixon, Paul *Northern Ireland: The Politics of War and Peace* (Basingstoke: Palgrave Macmillan, 2008); O'Donnell, Catherine, *Fianna Fáil, Irish Republicanism and the Northern Ireland Troubles, 1968–2005* (Dublin: Irish Academic Press, 2007); Tonge, Jonathan, *The New Northern Irish Politics?* (Basingstoke Palgrave Macmillan, 2005).

Index

A Beginner's Guide to Crimes Against Humanity

978-1-85168-601-8
£9.99/ $14.95

Using examples ranging from the genocides in Darfur and Rwanda to the use of torture in the 'war on terror,' Jones explores the progress made in toughening international law, and the stumbling blocks which prevent full compliance. Coherent and revealing, this book is essential for anyone interested in the well-being of humanity and its future.

"Jones has written a much-needed conceptual overview and call to action which will wake people up to the worst of which humanity is capable." **Charli Carpenter** – Assistant Professor, Department of Political Science, University of Massachusetts Amherst

"A remarkable book that is immediately accessible for the novice in the field, or students, and yet also engages with its topic in intellectually interesting ways for the more seasoned reader." **James Gow** – Professor of International Peace and Security, King's College London

ADAM JONES, Ph.D., is Associate Professor of Political Science at the University of British Columbia Okanagan, Canada.

A Beginner's Guide to The Middle East

The Middle East

9781851686759
£9.99/ $14.95

Organised thematically, and dealing with all the pivotal issues in the region, this comprehensive primer is both easy-to-read and full of insight. Stuffed with historical background, real-life examples, profiles of key figures and popular jokes from the area, it will captivate tourists, students, and the interested general reader alike.

"Masterly. A comprehensive and succinct overview." **Hugh Pope** – Former Middle East Correspondent for *Reuters, Wall Street Journal,* and the *Independent*

"The best book on the modern Middle East. Perfect not only for students but for any reader. It is balanced, authoritative and easy to follow. A perfect introduction to this troubled region." **Christopher Catherwood** – Author of *A Brief History of the Middle East*

PHIL ROBINS is Reader in Middle East Politics at the University of Oxford. He is the author of *A History of Jordan* and has previously worked as a journalist for the BBC and the *Guardian*.

Browse further titles at
www.oneworld-publications.com

Beginners
GUIDES

A Beginner's Guide to Civil Liberties

Tom Head traverses the globe in order to provide a clear introduction to what civil liberties are and why they're worth defending. This handy guide offers a fascinating global history of civil liberties paired with inspiring advice on how to take an active role in their defence -- before it's too late.

978-1-85168-644-5
£9.99/ $14.95

"The book interweaves history, philosophy, and much-needed practical advice for activists. Passing on his perspective, Tom's also given us a good read!" **Patricia Ireland** – activist and former president of NOW, the National Organization for Women

"A thought-provoking work. If enough people read it a, his observation that 'civil liberties have historically been a hypocrite's business' will no longer ring true." **Mike Newdow** – campaigner famous for his efforts to ban the phrase "under God" in the American Pledge of Allegiance

Author and activist **TOM HEAD** serves as civil liberties guide for About.com, a division of the New York Times Company.